Nicholas Monsarrat was born
of a distinguished surgeon. He
then at Trinity College, Camb.
He gave up law to earn a m   ...nce
journalist while he began writi.   ...s first novel to
receive significant attention was *This is the Schoolroom*
(1939). It is a largely autobiographical 'coming of age'
novel dealing with the end of college life, the 'Hungry
Thirties', and the Spanish Civil War.

During World War Two he served in the Royal Navy in
corvettes in the North Atlantic. These experiences were
used in his best-known novel, *The Cruel Sea* (1951) and
made into a film starring Jack Hawkins.

In 1946, he became a director of the UK Information
Service, first in Johannesburg, then in Ottawa. Other well-
known novels include *The Kapillan of Malta, The Tribe That
Lost Its Head*, and its sequel, *Richer Than All His Tribe*, and
The Story of Esther Costello.

He died in August 1979 as he was writing the second
part of his intended three-volume novel on seafaring life
from Napoleonic times to the present, *The Master Mariner*.

BY THE SAME AUTHOR
ALL PUBLISHED BY HOUSE OF STRATUS

HMS MARLBOROUGH WILL ENTER HARBOUR
LIFE IS A FOUR-LETTER WORD
THE MASTER MARINER
THE NYLON PIRATES
THE PILLOW FIGHT
RICHER THAN ALL HIS TRIBE
SMITH AND JONES
SOMETHING TO HIDE
THE SHIP THAT DIED OF SHAME
THE STORY OF ESTHER COSTELLO
THIS IS THE SCHOOLROOM
THE TIME BEFORE THIS
THE TRIBE THAT LOST ITS HEAD
THE WHITE RAJAH

Nicholas
Monsarrat

❖

H.M. FRIGATE

HOUSE OF
STRATUS

First published in 1946
Copyright © 1946-2013 Estate of Nicholas Monsarrat

All rights reserved. No part of this publication may be reproduced, stored in a retrieval system, or transmitted, in any form, or by any means (electronic, mechanical, photocopying, recording, or otherwise), without the prior permission of the publisher. Any person who does any unauthorised act in relation to this publication may be liable to criminal prosecution and civil claims for damages.

The right of Nicholas Monsarrat to be identified as the author of this work has been asserted in accordance with sections 77 and 78 of the Copyright, Designs and Patents Act 1988.

This edition published in 2013 by House of Stratus, an imprint of Stratus Books Ltd., Lisandra House, Fore Street, Looe, Cornwall, PL13 1AD, U.K.

www.houseofstratus.com

Typeset, printed and bound by House of Stratus.

A catalogue record for this book is available from the British Library.

ISBN 978-07551-425-8-3

This book is sold subject to the condition that it shall not be lent, re-sold, hired out, or otherwise circulated without the publisher's express prior consent in any form of binding, or cover, other than the original as herein published and without a similar condition being imposed on any subsequent purchaser, or bona fide possessor.

This is a fictional work and all characters are drawn from the author's imagination. Any resemblance or similarities are entirely coincidental.

LIST OF ILLUSTRATIONS

Bringing her alongside   7
She looked enormous   8
We were thus kept busy   23
We ran fourteen sea-trials   57
Frigate Alley   59
We practised action stations   62
In odd uniforms   63

ACKNOWLEDGEMENTS

A number of sentences describing British sailors in America and the story of the men under punishmen have been lifted from two articles of mine in the *Saturday Evening Post* and the *Atlantic Monthly*, respectively. To the editors of these journals I apologize for my laziness in borrowing instead of rewriting. But unwillingness to tamper with flawless jewels of prose undoubtedly entered in.

The frontispiece is reprinted by kind permission of James Kelley of the *Boston Herald*. The remaining photographs are Crown copyright, and permission to reproduce them is gratefully acknowledged.

N. M.

CHAPTER ONE

LEAVING AGAIN

It was a good party: farewell parties, when you are giving up one command and going on leave before the next one, usually are. We had managed to pack the Admiral and sixty-four assorted others into the wardroom by midday; and we did not sweep the last stayers off the quarter-deck till a quarter to three. (At one time the gin threatened to give out; but the guests, never.) The intervening hours seemed only just long enough to say goodbye to a number of people I was going to miss, after two years in ships attached to this base; and to introduce my successor in command of *Winger* to the various types who would make life a little easier and a lot more expensive for him in the future.

She was the third ship I had said goodbye to, and I wasn't growing to like the process; even if she had not been my first command, and especially cherished for that reason, I would have been sorry to leave such a lively and elegant companion. To say that all my past life in her flashed before my eyes would be untrue (though it would be an agreeable literary device for introducing a survey of all the convoys, patrols, dubious manoeuvres, and downright blunders which had made up the past seven months); but standing in the middle of that party's crush and uproar, which the

Admiral, I noticed, was viewing with a certain lack of enthusiasm, I did feel that this goodbye was not all fun.

The future had all sorts of possibilities, however; and to go back to the Atlantic, in a bigger and better ship, after two years of East Coast convoys, was just what I had been wanting to do.

I made the rounds, as far as I could in the crowd, and tried to see that everyone had a full glass and a contented expression and a share of a girl to talk to. At one point I found myself close to a Wren, a pretty girl with ambition and a correspondingly slight interest in naval officers of my rank. But she began, as she was in decency bound to, having a substantial glass of my gin in her hand, by asking me where I was going to next.

"A frigate," I told her.

"What's that?"

Falsely assuming that she really wanted to know: "A frigate," I began, "is an escort ship approximately the size of a destroyer, about two thousand tons, with nine officers and a hundred and forty men. They're really a development of the corvette, but—"

At this point an unsubtle yawn indicated that she was not interested, in the remotest degree, in frigates or corvettes: or, for that matter, in me. I tried something different (you can't just chuck your hand in, leaving no address).

"Do you know X?" I asked her.

She brightened immediately. "Oh, yes! He's just got his brass hat, hasn't he? Isn't it wonderful?"

I said yes, it certainly was, in a way, wonderful. (Someone at the club had remarked, on the other hand, that it was a hard blow for England, just when victory was coming in sight.) Something in my voice must have betrayed a lack of exhilaration, for she looked at the two and a half rings on my arm in a rather particular manner, and then said, "It must be difficult not to be jealous."

After that I gave up, and went and talked to the boys instead. Hell, I thought, this is a *farewell* party; I don't *have* to put up with anything.

The boys were an assorted lot – shore staff, fellow corvetteers, trawler skippers, forthright young men in command of destroyers, plodding mariners who had been minesweeping up and down the same stretch of channel for four years, with the same infinite care and accuracy: all the people who had made this base, during the past two years, a fine place to relax in, between trips. There was a lot of the Navy in that wardroom, the unspectacular side of the Navy which keeps the coast in running order but makes the headlines only in crummy little stories about the Coxswain's Christmas Cake or the Captain's Cat ("Trained to Detect Aircraft at Ten Thousand Feet"). Together with ocean convoy work, it was in point of fact the only sort of Navy I knew anything about; the ship I was going to command would be the biggest one I had ever boarded, and her job, convoy escort, had been my life for as long as I could remember. But it did not have to be spectacular, in order to be satisfying: battleships might have their tremendous actions, fleet destroyers their glamour, but we in our year-to-year concentration on the solid, enduring job of passing convoys through whatever lay in wait for them, had found in sea-going an anonymous pride of endeavour, as deeply stirring as any other brand.

Not that one ever thought of that, in so many words: and certainly not in the middle of an amiable shambles such as this ... I broke into a group of hardened mariners who were busy thrashing out the previous night's activities (the question of who had rammed who was obscure, but it didn't sound like the enemy) and became involved in speculation about my future sphere of operations which included the Caspian Sea and the Gulf of Alaska in its wide survey.

"But I suppose," said one of them, "that wherever it is, you'll go on writing those damned books of yours."

I said I would certainly do just that.

"You can start a new series now, can't you?—*H.M. Frigate, East Coast Frigate*, and all the rest."

I hadn't thought of it, I told him, but it might well be so.

He took a drink (*my* drink), and remarked: "*Japanese Frigate* will sound a bit exotic, don't you think?"

I went and talked to somebody else. I still felt confident of finding some cosy niche where I would be appreciated; but the guests seemed intent on only two things – punishing the wardroom wine stock and firing off one last telling crack before I finally got out of range.

The Commander (Signals) reminded me that in *other* theatres of operation they probably opened fire on ships which gave the wrong recognition signals, instead of being content with a mere verbal rebuke.

The Captain of a trawler which frequently came under me when on convoy duty, said he hoped that I myself would find out what it was like to be mucked about by another ship with two knots more speed and ten cents worth of seniority.

The Major who supervises (with gallantry of various kinds) the defence of the local coastline, asked me for a free copy of *H.M. Corvette* and said that he had *loved Destroyer from America* (by, as it happens, John Fernald).

The lovely Wren who ran the coal-boat beckoned me behind a depth-charge and said it was all very sad, but that my successor looked terribly interesting, and did I know his Christian name?

Even the Admiral (whose presence was a notable compliment to the ship) remarked on leaving that he had been coming down to the quay for lunch anyway.

Time passed.

Somewhere about two o'clock a destroyer going out on early patrol signalled: "Thanks for a grand party. Haven't they gone yet?" I had the signal copied out in quintuplicate and handed round the assembled company, but it made hardly any difference to them. I could not help feeling that their endurance and disregard of fatigue were worthy both of the finest traditions of the Service, and of a more profitable application elsewhere. They stayed, in fact, until the clatter of cutlery, made by a strong-minded steward with one eye on the liberty-boat and the other on our ruined lunch, developed into such a prodigious racket that it could no longer be ignored.

Even so, lunch was served for sixteen; and the train I finally caught bore no relation to the one in my proposed schedule.

In fact, it did not seem to bear much relation to a train of any sort.

CHAPTER TWO
ARRIVING AGAIN

The new ship, which I picked out by her pendant-numbers at about a hundred yards away, looked everything that a Western Approaches escort vessel should be; tough, weather-beaten, and workmanlike. She was the inside ship of a tier of three, all frigates; but she was only one of about thirty others secured stem to stern along the quayside; destroyers, sloops, corvettes, trawlers, rescue-tugs, all exhibiting much the same air of power and dependability. She fitted well into the picture, this ship of mine, but she was simply one unit in a big and tough outfit; for this was, obviously, a North Atlantic naval base in full flower, busy, overworked, and intent on the job, and that meant a lot of good ships in a very small space.

The impression of this concentrated activity, this trained and expert company, grew as I made my way down the quay. On the one side were the tiers of ships, their bows pointing seawards, their gangway sentries sloping arms and saluting as I passed; on the other were the various buildings and offices which helped them to get ready for sea or looked after them when they returned to harbour. They each had their respective labels, making a formidable catalogue of activity: Minesweeping Office, Depth-charge Driller, Accountant Office, Maintenance Captain, W/T,

Anti-Submarine Training Unit, Naval Stores, NAAFI Canteen, Torpedo Officer, Gunnery Stores – all the various sections which go to keep a ship afloat and alive. Nor was the space between them and the ships clear, by any means: both the offices and the ships had overflowed, spreading a jumble of wires, gangways, spare timber, boats under repair, sections of damaged and blasted plating, minesweeping gear, shell-cases, oil-drums, and dustbins.

I picked my way through them, dodging the dogs, cats, Wrens, bicycles, ships' postmen, working parties, lorries, and cranes, and noting the ships as I went by. Most of them I knew well, by name – they were the kind of ships which were always figuring in the reports of proceedings, as having rammed, sunk, demolished, or otherwise discouraged

Bringing her alongside.

U-boats all over the Atlantic; a few of them I knew personally, and marked down for a visit later. Aboard them, and alongside, was the usual daytime activity of ships in harbour; one was taking in stores, one exercising action stations, one oiling, one reading a punishment warrant to a square of expressionless seamen with a jaunty-looking culprit in the centre. Approximately one in every three had paint-stages rigged over the side, and was beautifying herself; and every single one, without exception, had the same hoist of flags close up to the yardarm – there was an exercise in progress, and the Yeomen of Signals were going to it with a will … It was all familiar, and somehow comforting: demonstrating, not that the Navy Never Sleeps (on the contrary, it gets its head down, fathoms deep, on

She looked enormous.

every possible occasion), but that this section of the Navy is the hardest working and the most highly trained of all.

And this ship, my ship, was part of it ... She looked enormous, close to; the tide was high, and she seemed to tower above the jetty, building up steeply from quarterdeck, foc'sle, flag deck, bridge, upper bridge, crow's nest, and W/T aerial, to a single odd-looking bit of equipment at the masthead, which might have been anything from an electric toaster to a parrot-cage. (I would have to ask what it was, a little later.) That impression of size increased as I boarded her and was led by an alert Officer-of-the-Day towards the wardroom companionway: she was over three hundred feet long (a hundred feet longer than a corvette) and she had about her a solid air, a feeling of toughness and strength, to which her formidable armament and immense outfit of depth-charges further testified.

Later, of course, when I got used to handling her, I hardly noticed her size at all, except to be glad that she could stand up to the weather so well; but at the beginning (on the second afternoon, for example, when we had to shift our berth a few places downstream) I was conscious of it all the time. Everything weighed heavy, everything was a little longer and wider than I had reckoned for: she was slower to start, and harder to stop, and the amount of wind resistance presented by her hull was an impressive element which had to be taken into account continuously. Bringing her alongside the quay again, that first time, was rather like moving a block of flats two hundred yards down the road, using supernatural powers but only human judgment. After my honeymoon with the slim and subtle *Winger*, this was Darby-and-Joan stuff with a far stouter party. Two thousand two hundred tons can't be disguised by a few frills and a riveted brassiere.

Her name, incidentally, was H.M.S. *River:* she was Tyne-built, and just six months old; and she had spent all that time on Atlantic convoy duty, in an escort group with something of a reputation for team-work and efficiency. She was thus a notable responsibility: on that first day, looking round the ships in company and remembering their record, I felt just about capable of taking her on, and not much more.

But at the same time I could not help remembering that this feeling of a personal ordeal in the near future had recurred with each successive step upwards in the Navy. It lent an edge to promotion, and it was a powerful stimulant; but it never lasted long. The higher standard of awareness and skill became, inevitably, the routine measure of what was necessary.

I had, certainly, a strong team to back me up on this present occasion. The First Lieutenant, an R.N.R. officer with over three years' seniority, introduced the other officers to me a little later that afternoon: the rest of the wardroom consisted of another lieutenant as Gunnery Officer, an R.N.R. sub as Navigator, three other sub-lieutenants, a midshipman, the Engineer Officer and two other engineering subs who were borne for training, and the Surgeon Lieutenant. They were a young lot, of course – the average age, excluding myself and the Chief, was just over twenty-three: but their collective experience (some of it on the lower deck) was impressive – Atlantic escort, Home Fleet destroyers, North Africa landing, Russian convoys (the toughest of the lot, to date), East Coast mine-dodging, the West African station – anything in fact, from sweltering to freezing, with danger, boredom, and prolonged hardship in between. Guns was a New Zealander who had not been home for over three years: the engineering subs were Canadians, and tough at that. Altogether, three of them held watch-keeping tickets, and the others had already reached the stage of wondering why they didn't – to my mind a very healthy stage indeed.

The fact that the ship carried a doctor, presiding over a beautifully equipped sick bay with two sick berth attendants to help him, gave one a distinct feeling of superiority as well as being a solid comfort in the background: it recalled, to me, the makeshifts of the old days in corvettes, when I myself was charged with this job, for the sole reason that my father was a surgeon and it was thought that I might have inherited some of his skill. It recalled the crude aftermath of U-boat attacks and torpedoings – the rough bandaging of gross lacerations, the surgical stitching undertaken for the first time on any stage – the stage being a dim rocking mess-deck crowded with half-drowned, oil-drenched survivors: the dead men who might have been alive to-day if I had had more knowledge or more nerve. That was all past now, thank God: I suppose it was good for the soul to learn quickly, but not, perhaps, as quickly as that.

With twelve officers and a crew of a hundred and forty, the ship, for all her size, was crowded – that was the chief impression I had later, when I walked round with Number One. The mess-decks were well planned and roomy, for this class of ship; but wartime increases in complement resulting from additional technical equipment had, as usual, turned hammock-swinging into a close-set jig-saw pattern and brought locker-space down to the minimum.

The chief petty officers' mess, for example, had been invaded by E.R.A.s who now outnumbered them three-to-one: extra Radar and W/T ratings had stirred the seamen into a pretty thick mixture. It was inevitable, bearing in mind the extraordinarily complex weapon which the modern escort vessel has become; but it did not make life at sea in bad weather any more tolerable, or harbour periods much of a relief from discomfort. I could only hope that it did not make for too much bickering, or cause divisional officers too many headaches.

A note on the divisional system may not be out of place for those readers who are unfamiliar with it: it is, to my mind, the Navy's most admirable organization, and if the other services have no parallel to it, that is probably what is wrong with them. ... Briefly, a ship's company is divided into "divisions", according to the various branches – seamen, stokers, communications, etc.: each group of men has an officer to look after it, an officer specifically charged with its welfare and regulation. It is to him they look in all their difficulties, whether concerned with promotion, training for a higher rate, doubts about their pay, internal quarrels and problems, domestic complications, compassionate leave, complaints of unfairness or favouritism. This division into small groups, if conscientiously applied, makes for a high degree of confidence between officers and men: officers can get to know their men far more easily, and can gauge their capabilities, ratings can feel that they have, in their divisional officer, a friend and a personal adviser as well as a disciplinarian.

It is a demonstration, continuously apparent to everyone on the lower deck, that authority is not just a vague group of "higher-ups", too busy to care about their troubles, too strict to be challenged on any point, and too remote to talk to. It is something I believe in whole-heartedly, as a vital safeguard in a regime which many outsiders think is totally authoritarian. It is nothing of the sort: the divisional system gives that the he. But it must be taken conscientiously, by the whole wardroom, if it is to have its full effect.

As I wrote later in my standing orders: "I want the term 'divisional officer' to mean a great deal in this ship, both to officers and ratings. Officers should take the utmost personal and professional interest in the men in their division: ratings should be made to feel that they have a willing advocate as well as a strict disciplinarian, in their divisional officer. As a minimum, officers should know the following about every rating in their division: his capacity for work, his trustworthiness, his chances of promotion, his date for the next Good Conduct Badge or progressive pay, a rough idea of his home life and background, and his more pressing worries if any."

A digression: but, to me, an agreeable one ... After the mess-decks I had a brief look round the engine-room, which the boiler-clean and repair period had rendered something less than orderly. But just as the size of *River* had conveyed an idea of toughness, so down here the row upon row of gauges and the big twin turbines suggested a comforting reserve of power and speed. Frigates (as I had tried to explain to the unenthusiastic Wren at the party) are a development of the corvette, but they are more than an improvement on a highly successful design: they embody the new idea of a powerful "self-reliant" ship as big as a destroyer, a few knots slower but with far greater range, and carrying the last word in antisubmarine equipment: a ship, that is, designed to be the tough nucleus of an escort group rather than a rank-and-file member of it.

I believe my friend "M" (from *H.M. Corvette)* was the first R.N.V.R. officer to command one: I was the second, being beaten by a week or so. If we had been told, as subs in H.M.S. *Flower,* that such a command would eventually come our way, it might well have permanently affected our outlook – and with it our careers. It is perhaps just as well that at that stage we had no greater ambition than to earn our watch keeping tickets and get the cyphers to come out right.

The wardroom, which I looked at next, was in much the same state of overcrowding as the mess-decks: two of the subs had to eat at a separate table, and the competition for the sofa at the end of a meal recalled the after-dinner rush at a residential hotel, with the guests wolfing their food, streaking for the lounge, and suffering agonies of indigestion as a consequence. Incidentally, the allowance of three stewards for twelve officers seemed inadequate by any except hash-house standards: in harbour it meant one dishing up, one ashore on liberty, and one to serve the whole meal on his own. Wartime austerity was much in evidence as regards the furnishing – bleak iron radiators instead of a stove, and chairs of that modern tubular design which makes the "shape of things to come" so morbid a prospect. But as the wardroom of a fighting ship built in the fifth year of war, it was far from being discreditable: if the designers had concentrated more on the ship's fighting qualities than on her comfort, as seemed to be the case, that could hardly be put on the debit side of the balance.

My own cabin, with a bathroom attached, was a big one, and adequately comfortable: though here again the wartime finish was apparent – it had none of *Winger's* elegance in the form of polished woodwork or cushioned chairs. But it was, all the same, imposing enough to mark the step-up in the social scale, if I had any time to ponder distinctions of such subtle triviality.

River's upper deck was a heartening sight, even in the state of partial dissolution which a boiler-clean entailed. She had approximately double the fire-power of a corvette, with lashings of ready-use ammunition lockers, and power-operated hoists from the magazines; and her full complement of depth-charges made one blink one's eyes. The impression was, again, one of solidity and strength: in a corvette the Oerlikon and two-pounder mountings made an appreciable difference to the top-weight, here they could be planted almost at will, like candles in a birthday cake of the pre-war, majestic sort. This ship was a steadfast platform, for guns, for men, for fighting enterprise or rocklike endurance; the sort of ship a sailor likes to have beneath his feet.

And heavily armed as she was, there still seemed to be

plenty of elbow-room for working wires and tackles: a different story from the old-style corvette, where for instance two or three hands had to stand *inside* the galley when tailing onto the depth-charge hoist, and getting in the seaboat entailed leading the falls through a positive maze of blocks. Here there was room to do things in style, and sufficient, incidentally, to give me an uninterrupted afternoon walk of at least a hundred feet, right on my own front doorstep.

I went up to the bridge last of all: it was a pleasure I had been keeping in reserve, and I was not disappointed. There was no wartime austerity here: it was as well-equipped and finished as any I had seen, with a system of inter-communication between the various parts of the ship which (I could see) was going to take some time to master. (It is all right in daylight: it is in the pitch dark that one must be able to assess the urgency of a report from the voice-pipe that relays it, to put one's hand unerringly on an alarm-gong or a "stand by" buzzer, to know, for instance, that a phone ringing just in front of you is a message from "A" gun, and another one, dimly heard from inside the asdic cabinet, means a breakdown report from the quarter-deck. Seconds before the actual message is given you, it may be time to envisage a new situation or make a vital alteration of plan.)

From this bridge, once I had it in a tight grip, command could be fittingly exercised ... It was of the authentic destroyer type: open, properly shielded by glass dodgers, with batteries of voice-pipes and telephones lining two sides of it, and a grand array of instruments – asdic repeater, log, compass, gunnery indicators, and other more discreet products – on the forward end. My chair was centrally placed, high up behind the gyro-compass: there was a solid chart-table close at hand, and a view of the plot (an instrument for recording the ship's movements as she goes along, by means of a track-chart) without walking twenty yards and turning two corners to get it. The flag-deck and signalling platform were separately sited, well clear of the main stream of activity; and there was, to finish it off, a covered approach leading up from the sea-cabin. (That had been the curse of *Winger's* bridge: aboard her, you stepped out of the sea-cabin straight onto the upper-deck – always on the weather side, always wet and windswept, and destroying all dreams of home and calculations of pay in one sudden cold douche.)

I nodded appreciatively to Number One. "Very nice," I said. "What are the drawbacks?"

His humorous face curved into a grin. "It's extraordinarily draughty at sea, sir," he answered. "That dodger is more for looks than for action. And the chart-table canopy has leaked ever since she was built: in winter we ruin about one folio of charts per trip. But I think the whole thing is pretty well planned, all the same."

"Who is up here, at cruising stations?"

"Signalman, two look-outs, bridge messenger, and spare asdic operator, sir." He reeled them off competently. "The quartermaster, one telegraph hand, and the bosun's mate are below in the wheelhouse, and the Petty Officer of the Watch spends most of his time there too." Pointing aft along the upper deck, he went into details of guns'-crews, look-outs, and depth-charge parties. "They're spread a bit thin in the daytime, of course," he concluded, "but that's the only way I can work the hands in three watches.[1] We're pretty well off at full action stations."

That "I" in his phrase "I can work the hands" was one of the first signs I had that this First Lieutenant knew his job. (There were to be many others.) A good First Lieutenant

---

[1] i.e., working four hours on and eight off, the only possible method except for very short trips.

should feel, all the time, a *personal* responsibility for the ship's organization: there can be no collective authority to fall back on where he is concerned. If he had said: "*We* can't do it any other way," or shown anything except a conviction of direct personal control, I would have suspected that he was probably ready to share his job with other officers, or put his problems onto a vague impersonal basis which somehow excused their solution.

I had learnt the lesson myself, in a single exchange of sentences, when I was First Lieutenant of *Dipper*. I had remarked to the Captain, casually: "I doubt if we can get the ship's side painted by Tuesday," and had received the forthright reply: "Do you mean you and God? There's no one else responsible, as far as I know."

I had thought that a little rough at the time, as I had used the word "we" almost unconsciously; but it was, in fact, the unconscious which was at fault – I had betrayed the idea, in the back of my mind, that my inability to finish painting could somehow be shared out among seven officers and eighty-eight men, and that was what the Captain had seized on. In point of fact, the ship's side was my responsibility alone: if it was unfinished, it was for me to explain why, with a full acknowledgment that it was *my* job which was uncompleted.

I spent the rest of the evening with Number One in my cabin, discussing the very many things involved in taking over the ship. Once again (it had happened with *Winger*) the last Captain had gone sick before I arrived, and I would not get a direct turn-over from him – a rather woolly situation, with nothing signed for and, of course, lacking that clear picture of the ship which only a man who had commanded her for six months could give me. But there was so little time to worry about that side of it that I could only take it in my stride. No comforting pause would ensue, no gentle easing into the job: the hands returned from leave that night, and our programme was to start next morning – three days' harbour drills, four days, sea exercises with the rest of the escort group, and then straight out on a transatlantic convoy.

Later, sitting alone in my cabin, I was much startled by a sudden uproar of whistles and sirens from all over the harbour, and I jumped for my steel helmet – where I came from, that was the crash alarm for imminent air attack. But it was only ships in company giving a suitable welcome to the New Year ... Have I described, adequately, how superior I thought my New Year's present was? Probably not: I doubt if a string of first impressions can give anything except a vague picture; the rest must emerge later, from day to day. And certainly it cannot convey the pride I felt in this new command, which put me back where I wanted to be – in a grand ship, in the North Atlantic, in the forefront of a winning battle.

That was a good New Year.

If that naval base took any holidays, the New Year's Day was not one of them. From 8.45 next morning, by which grisly hour I was ashore and about to embark on a complicated "game" of escort tactics, the time was as full and as crowded as it could be: one felt one had been drawn into a remorseless machine which then set to work on ships and men, making them fit and ready (as far as intensive training could) for the fight at sea. That base was an astonishing place in many ways: a square mile or so centred round the quay, concentrated and dedicated to the one idea – the winning of the struggle in the North Atlantic. Nothing was left out of account: as well as taking in hand anything affecting the equipment side of ship's efficiency, it covered training classes, practices of all kinds, lectures, sea and harbour exercises, examinations – a complete curriculum designed to tune up officers and men, and to discover any weak points in a ship's organization, before it was put to the test.

The full work-out, which every ship received, every time in harbour, was inclined to be an exhausting process. Three days' harbour drills, followed by four days' sea exercises – everything from towing a "captured" submarine to night shoots – and all the time the daily routine and the complex paper-work in the background, meant very little spare time. It was a relief to fire the last shot, polish off the last report, sign the last receipt, and go off to sea for a rest.

But there was a lot to learn, even simply to keep up with new ideas and inventions; and for me personally, after two years of coastal convoy work, there was an enormous amount of leeway to make up. The Atlantic I was returning to was a very different place from the one I had left: the rather haphazard escort methods of the early days – tremendously hard work, long endurance, moderate skill, and little science – had no place now, in a job which had been organized and sharpened into a lethal routine. Guesswork, the old-fashioned wooden asdic (as a friend of mine used to call it), the feeling which is summed up in the phrase "It'll be all right on the night" – these had gone the way of all improvisations, and had been replaced, through the intensive struggles of the past years, by the application of new tactics, by technical skill of a high order, and by weapons on which ceaseless experiment as well as tremendous ingenuity had been lavished.

It was, perhaps, in the operational sphere that the biggest advances had been made: there now seemed to be a well-considered routine for every eventuality, and a triumphant precedent for most of them; but there was no doubt that the whole theatre was better organized, technically more complex, tactically more accomplished.

It was also much more successful. Gone, once again, were the old days, when the regular loss of four or five ships on every convoy was accepted as an inevitable toll. Gone were the hard years such as 1941, when a total of 892 British ships were lost: gone were the ruthless pack-attacks, the dogged shadowing by long-range aircraft which were on our trail almost before we cleared harbour, the formidable game of hide-and-seek whose rules seemed to be cruelly weighted against us.

Now the sides were reversed: we were no longer the hunted – or, if we were, it was a hunt pursued with a diminishing enterprise which the first tough counter-blow seemed to demolish. That sort of thing was now happening time and again: the U-boats coming in for an attack, being frustrated before their effort was well in train, and thereupon giving up and going off in search of an easier quarry. This was certainly new: in the old days, the idea of a U-boat retiring for a bath and a shave after one single crack at a convoy would have seemed preposterous.

Something was lacking – the thrusting morale, the old Teutonic spite; and something new had been added on our side – a feeling of confidence, a flowing enterprise, which made *us* the hunters. True, not all the U-boat onslaughts were fruitless: there was an occasional vicious flare-up which took toll of merchant ships or escorts; but this was, over all, a cleansed and victorious Atlantic – many times, as the monthly statistics showed, our U-boat sinkings outnumbered the merchant ships we lost – and to return to it now, in this splendid ship, was a tremendous tonic.

We went down river at dusk, the evening before the convoy sailed, to top up with oil and to be ready for an early start; and when the group was settled at anchor the Senior Officer summoned a conference, of captains and navigating officers, on board his ship.

It was a time for questions, for last-minute arrangements, for the allocation of R/T call-signs and the settling of signal routines: a final review of the prospects before we went into action, and the last chance to settle our doubts, if we had any which the previous days' training had left unanswered. We sat round a table in that destroyer's attractive wardroom, with its polished stove and its comfortable old-fashioned furniture: a table littered with charts, sailing directions, convoy lists, group orders, signal books and pads – all the essential oddments which would, at sailing time to-morrow, be taken up to the bridge, where they would remain throughout the trip.

The morrow would work a change in ourselves, too, turning us into memorized pendant numbers and odd-sounding call-signs instead of names and faces; but tonight we were still individuals—a muster of young and not-so-young men (the eldest a commander of fifty, the youngest a Canadian two-ringer of twenty-three), drawn from all sorts of occupations, trained for years together at this one job, and now discharging, with the necessary skill and awareness, the responsibility of command. We all had much the same air, I suppose, in a greater or less degree: an air of purpose, of knowing what this was all about, of tiredness waiting to overtake us in the background. We all had faces a little more lined than they should have been, a certain lack of gaiety, and rather a lot of grey hairs. Sea-going is always a wearing business: command, in wartime, is the most wearing of all; and looking round the faces of that pre-escort conference, it was easy to see how faithfully this process was mirrored in line and expression, and to be aware, without undue self consciousness, of oneself as the same slightly battered reflection. If anyone asks me what I did in the second Great War, I can at least answer: "I ruined my chances of going on the films."

We talked, and listened, and went into private conference with the man who would be nearest to us on the escort screen, and thought now and then about getting a good night's sleep, before the start of the trip. But finally it was over, and the group-commander, gathering up a sheaf of papers and handing them over to his secretary, sat back and said: "That's the lot, I think. I won't recapitulate, because I think we've got it all clear. But there are just three things I want you to bear in mind all the time, and I'll run through those. The first is communications. I want these to be right on the top line, every hour of the day and night. Acknowledge signals straight away: if you don't know the answer, or can't make up your mind, or want to look it up in the book, say so – the thing I *don't* want is a blank silence, so that I don't know whether my signal has got through or not.

"The second thing is to keep me informed, all the time, about what you're doing, if it's the smallest degree out of the ordinary. Unless I hear to the contrary, I always assume that you're plodding along quietly in your proper position: if you make a move without telling me and the other escorts, you're liable to get beaten up by your own side, and that's entirely your own fault. There's no room for guesswork on this job, especially on a dark night when all hell can break loose at a moment's notice."

"The last thing is personal initiative. You all know what I feel about that. You're in command of your ships, and free to handle them in the way you think best, providing it fits in with any overall scheme I may want to put in hand. If you see the need for quick action, don't waste time asking me if you can carry on with it. Make your signal: '*Intend to do so-and-so*' – I'll soon haul you back if I don't like it." He smiled. "Don't forget that you might be giving *me* a bright idea, just by starting something off your own bat ... And that really *is* all, I think." He looked across at me suddenly. "Are you quite happy about all this?"

I said that I was.

"Some of it is new, I know," he said, "but we had a good work-up together, and that should have given you the hang of it ... Now let's have a drink before we turn in."

The wind was rising as we came out on deck, and our

We were thus kept busy.

motor-boats, clustered round the boom, were jerking to a choppy swell. Pilot, preceding me down the ladder, lifted his face and sniffed the air.

"Something on the way," he remarked thoughtfully. "And I don't think it's the first day of spring."

That turned out to be a good guess.

CHAPTER THREE

TRANS-OCEAN ONE

What *was* on the way was a roaring westerly gale, which set in twelve hours later, just gave us time to get the convoy into shape before battering it to bits again, and lasted for six days on end.

I began by enjoying it. *River* was the obvious ship to use for running errands and rounding up the convoy at the start – she had the extra speed needed, and plenty of fuel to spare: we were thus kept busy as canteen-boat for most of the first day. It was a delight to handle her, in the various jobs which came our way – passing instructions to late arrivals, chivvying the stragglers, acting as the link between the rear escorts and the leader; and as we sped up and down the columns in the rising sea, *River* demonstrated a manoeuvrability and a reserve of power which opened up a cheerful prospect. With this command I seemed to have graduated into a different class altogether: the ship behaved as well as she looked, and that was saying a lot. But with her good looks and her power went a lot of other things, things inherent in the "idea" of a frigate – more responsibility, more difficult jobs, the knowledge that a group-commander counted on a higher standard of efficiency and trustworthiness from this sort of ship than from the general run of escorts.

On that first day, when the errands we ran had to be completed with the minimum of fuss and waste of time, against the rising wind and sea, and the disorganization these would shortly induce, one was conscious of this test of responsibility; and looking down on the dripping fo'c'sle, feeling the thrust of her bows as she shouldered one wave and then went right through the next one, watching the shipped water surge aft, jolt against "X" gun platform, and cascade onto the quarter-deck, I knew that failure to meet this test would be my fault and not the ship's.

She was a weapon well fitted to induce this sort of knowledge; and well able to promote the necessary confidence too.

It was odd, and relieving, to see so much water around us again: this was the most generous amount of sea-room I had had for about two years. All the time on the East Coast, wherever one looked at any hour of the day or night, there had always been something to catch the eye and something to worry about – a stretch of coastline, a buoy marking a spit of sand, the mast of a wreck sticking up. Now, beyond the convoy, there was nothing but hundreds of miles of free ocean – no shoals, no minefields, no tight corners where one might or might not be able to turn: nothing but what travel agents call the limitless blue, Homer the wine-dark, serpent-haunted sea, and sailors the drink.

The convoy was well in shape by the first day's dusk, moving slowly, thrusting against the mounting sea like an armoured spearhead treading down an enemy only just weaker than itself; by now the wind, veering from south to west, had a formidable weight in it, and coming up from astern at speed to take up our night station was an uncomfortable and very wet operation. That discomfort increased, though we eased down as soon as we were in position: the wind rose in fury as the hours passed, until by midnight it was blowing half a gale, and *River* was putting up a wild performance. Ordinarily she was a good sea-boat, as I had already discovered, but on this occasion she had too much to deal with altogether: though she rolled more slowly than a corvette she was just as good at it really, and all that night we were chucked about as brutally as I ever remembered. It blew harder and harder, with an astonishing intermittent howl which seemed to have a personal malice in it: it was impossible to see more than a few yards ahead, impossible to dodge the wind, impossible to find a secure position as the bridge rocked through an enormous arc and the raw spray came over in great spinning clouds.

I spent most of the night on the bridge, as sleep was out of the question, and I was in any case rather worried about our position in relation to the ships around us. The convoy was in a mess: one could almost *feel* it losing its cohesion and relapsing gradually into disorder; ships were all over the place, and the few that we occasionally saw were plugging along independently, intent only on keeping clear of trouble. When dawn came up at last, with the gale at its height, there was virtually nothing else in sight at all: a big tanker wallowing astern with two of its boats smashed in, and a sullen-looking Liberty ship far away to leeward, both of them dimly seen through the scud and often lost altogether, were all we had on our plate.

By midday, after some chatter over the R/T, and a few prudent excursions here and there, it was clear that the convoy was already scattered over at least forty miles, and likely to lose even that loose pattern unless things improved.

Things did not improve. It is easy to write about bad weather on this job: there is so much of it; often there has seemed to be nothing else throughout an entire winter – all other engagements are cancelled. But this first trip really was a winner in this respect. We had those head-winds, continuing at gale force, for almost the whole of the next six days: the convoy (for want of a better word) crawled along, scattered and out of reach, nosing into the wind and sea with a dull enduring apathy; at the end of a week we were a bare two hundred miles of our journey to the good, and when the weather moderated there might be days of crawling speed before the convoy formed up again. It was intensely tiring – the noise, the rolling, the hours of concentration on the bridge, when the difference between good and bad ship-handling, between control and carelessness, might be lost deck-gear, smashed boats, even the ship in danger of foundering. For the storm *was* as bad as that: three of the ships had to put back, badly damaged, and one of them came very near to sinking before she reached shelter. We were cold and wet, and short of sleep, nearly all the time: most of the officers' cabins, mine among them, were flooded out, and the mess-decks were the usual miserable shambles for days on end. In between times, I thought of the boys on their nice comfortable East Coast patrol, and wondered why I had ever got ambitious; but there was little time for that sort of philosophizing, and not much inclination either. I broke a rib the second day out – and I didn't do it laughing either: I was thrown out of my bunk, by a rather special wave, in the good old-fashioned way just like you read about in books, and brought up short against the opposite bulkhead. (That wave cost us one of the Carley life-rafts, which rolled right under and did not come up again.) Even though the doctor wired me up like a carnation, in reams of adhesive bandage, it meant a period of increasing pain until, by the twelfth day, it was practically a hundred per cent. But that was all of a piece with the rest of that trip, somehow.

When the weather moderated, on the seventh day, and the rolling eased to an occasional twenty-degree lurch, we were faced with the job of squaring up the ship and helping to reform the convoy. The first assignment was the easier: the glistening decks dried off, the mess-decks were baled out and tidied up, the smashed gear was repaired or ditched; within the space of a forenoon the ship had lost her battered air and was fit for the next round. But regaining touch with the other escorts, and rounding up the scattered merchant ships, was not so simple: it entailed two days and more of running to and fro, passing courses and speeds to puzzled stragglers, chasing over the horizon after independent spirits who wanted to cure their hang-overs in solitude; it meant wasting time, oil, and effort on guesswork which did not always turn out to be right.

There was one occasion when we joined up with another escort whom we encountered several miles astern of the convoy after one of these excursions; she was steering an odd course which, according to our calculations, would not take her anywhere special, but she seemed to know where she was going and I presumed that she was either in contact with the main body of the convoy, or had had a signal (which we had missed) about its altering course. It came as rather a shock, therefore, after running neck and neck with her for the best part of four hours without encountering anything, when she called us up and asked: "Why are we steering this course, please?"

The honest answer to that was that I didn't know, and that in another five minutes I would have asked the same question myself. But that didn't seem a very good reply to make in the circumstances, so we evaded the whole issue by a vague reference to "final rounding-up of stragglers", and shortly afterwards turned off in a more reasonable direction. She followed, with scarcely justified confidence. Luckily it turned out to be right.

There was another, even worse time, when after a long chase to the northward we caught up with a ship steering quite the wrong way – east instead of west, in fact – and tried to convince her that she would never find the convoy that way. She was a foreigner, and (we thought) exceptionally slow on the uptake … It transpired, after we had circled her like an anguished puppy for nearly an hour and put out a good deal of oratory on the loud-hailer, that she was a straggler from another convoy altogether, and bound independently for England. If a grey-camouflaged warship can ever be said to blush, *River* did just that.

But gradually our convoy got into shape again, in spite of diversions such as these. It was a wearisome business, hard on the patience, and we were very glad when every ship was accounted for, and more or less in its assigned position. We signalled to the group-commander that the convoy was reformed, added some technical information about the relative length of the columns, and took up our position on the screen. And then the whole thing happened again. That second storm, which once more scattered the convoy and undid all the work of the past two days, induced a fatalistic attitude which was probably the only way to meet it; but the situation could hardly have been more dispiriting. Here we were, already eight days out, with hardly anything to show for it in the way of distance run; and now for the second time the gale was dispersing the ships, throwing *River* about like a ponderous cork, and putting us through yet another tiring ordeal. This time it was not so long-continued: in fact the main force spent itself within two days; but it came at the wrong time, as far as morale was concerned, and it was just as effective in spoiling the look of the convoy and piling up work for us in the future. As we wallowed onwards, sometimes in touch with other ships, sometimes alone on a grey waste of water, and always cold and wet and tired, we began to feel that perhaps after all this convoy had got out of bed the wrong side at the very beginning, and would never regain a normal disposition. Or, as it was put by the Yeoman of Signals (not an outstandingly religious man): "I reckon Jonah would have been ditched long ago, on this trip."

Once more we squared things up as soon as a respite was given us, once more we raced around and ploughed to and fro, on the job of whipping in; and then, while I was still hesitating to send a "convoy reformed" signal to the group-commander, for fear of tempting providence again, action intervened from an unexpected quarter.

We picked up an S.O.S. – "ATTACKED BY SUBMARINE" from an unidentified merchant ship, a message which set us rather a puzzle. She couldn't be one of ours, as they were all accounted for: attempts to get in touch with her later produced no answer, and we had no means of knowing whether it was a genuine cry for help or a decoy-signal from a U-boat. The position given was 'way astern of the convoy, and up to the north: it might conceivably be the east-bound merchantman we had spoken to four days previously; but it didn't seem likely that she had made so little progress in the interval, with the roaring gale astern of her and no set speed to conform to. The situation was doubtful enough for the escort-commander to refer it to the Commander-in-Chief before taking any action; but after a wireless cross-talk, and a check with other convoys on passage, he was ordered to detach two ships to search the area and see what they could find.

The ships detached were ourselves, and a tough-looking destroyer by the name of *Falconer*. She gave us a rendezvous well clear of the convoy, and when we had established contact with her we set off together, at a speed which I hoped the Chief would agree to keep up without bursting into tears.

That was a singularly trying excursion, with a companion who went much too fast for our comfort, and in weather not greatly improved and growing progressively colder hour by hour. We made a quick slogging passage to the area indicated in the S.O.S. message; and then, after a bout of arithmetic which *Falconer* was good enough to ask me to check, we began an elaborate search. That didn't last long: in fact nothing lasted long, except the icy wind with its occasional drifts of snow, and the main outlines of this curious operation – scouring the ocean at eighteen knots in foul weather, and exchanging sardonic signals as we were (a) told to extend the search ninety miles to the northward; (b) recalled half-way because the weather grew too bad for any boats to be still afloat; (c) sent off again when it moderated, and (d) told to stay there for forty-eight hours whatever happened, the S.O.S. being thought to be bogus and a submarine ruse suspected. The gale came on again: the wind and the sea rose, the snow scudded over the bridge in whirling grey clouds: the track-chart began to look like a child's drawing of a flash of lighting; *River* signalled to *Falconer*, "The wild goose we are chasing seems to be getting quite out of control," and *Falconer*, easing down to secure some shifting oil-drums, signalled to *River*, "Some say Good old Max!" ...[2]

Of course, basically speaking, no one minded at all, when the operation was seen in the light of what might be at stake – a sinking ship, or men in open boats adrift in the chaos of those miserable days and nights. But with not much evidence of this to go on, and the weather making each change of plan a little more intolerable each time, good humour had to be helped out by an occasional assertion of the spirit.

There *was* something there, though, and I'm glad to say that we found it, when the forty-eight hours were nearly spent and we had completed a widening, crisscross search down-wind in the most bitter weather imaginable. It was about ten o'clock in the forenoon, and we were due to turn back at midday, when one of the lookouts spotted it – the stern half of a ship, floating sluggishly at an angle of about

---

[2] Possibly a friendly reference to Admiral Sir Max Horton, Commander-in-Chief, Western Approaches.

forty-five degrees to the level of the sea, the bows probably blown off by a torpedo and the remainder looking as if it had been shelled or had been on fire not long before. We had been expecting *something*, since from dawn that morning we had been passing successive patches of fresh wreckage – ladders and hatches and oddments of rope; but not something so hopelessly forlorn as this …

We had hardly made out 'what it was when it was blotted out altogether, by a blinding snowstorm which drove across the water like a fast-falling curtain. I remember very clearly that scene, which seemed to contain the elements of tragedy in strange, distorted miniature: *Falconer* and ourselves, the sole witnesses, nosing round the derelict at slow speed, the half-ship riding the waves at that ruined angle, the snow which drew a shroud over the whole thing, as though ashamed of the cruelty of man to man; and above all the unreality pervading this curious seascape, heightened by the knowledge that there was probably a submarine watching the whole thing from quite close to … I took a wide sheer outwards, to present a lesser target and avoid colliding with *Falconer*: immediately we were alone, curtained by snow, cut off from the party which had suddenly taken this disgusting turn. We were once more in a clean world, white and old-fashioned and pretty; smiles, and a Christmas forgiveness, screened the dirty outer edges.

But the snow passed, and presently the picture was restored. It was unhappy as well as ugly: clearly we had arrived too late, by two or three days. In accordance with our prearranged plan *Falconer* went in for a close look, while I screened the operation: we both fired guns and sounded whistles to attract attention, but nothing stirred on board – there was no one left alive there, nor, in that livid cold, could there have been anyone alive in any small boat which got away. The incident, as it stood, was complete and final.

A further signal from the Admiralty, that we were to

search for survivors and remain in the area to the limit of our fuel endurance, decided our next move; and after *Falconer* had sunk the derelict with some very handy gunnery we set off again on our zig-zag travels. We were looking for two things – open boats, and the submarine that had done the damage; and it was obvious that the latter was the more likely to be met with. Even if the ship had managed to get any boats away in the storm of three days ago, they could hardly be still afloat now. On board, we were very much alert: the sight of the torpedoed ship had been like a sudden injection, charging the normal monotony of convoy escort with the drama and hazard of war: the Atlantic battle *wasn't* over, there *were* still submarines at work and there was one not very far away which had demonstrated the fact with all the old ruthlessness. Our chances of finding her were not good: she was not likely to have stayed in the area unless she was spoiling for a fight, and knowing that the recent storm might have scattered a number of other convoys and produced plenty of lone stragglers like her last victim, she might well prefer to look for easier prey than a vengeful escort ship on the prowl.

On the other hand, success sometimes has odd results. In this case it might be such a morale-raiser that the U-boat was prepared to hang about and try to knock off any rescuers who might appear – and as this thought struck me, a disagreeable noise came up the engine-room voice-pipe, the main switch-board blew out, and the ship came to a dead stop.

I had been stopped before in mid-Atlantic, but never quite as completely as this. Snow drifting down a ventilator shaft had caused the trouble, and it was trouble of a basic sort. Through that switch-board went every circuit in the ship: when it burnt out, the lights failed, the gyro-compass went dead, the boiler-room fans stopped (and with them, of course, the main steam supply), and the radio and internal communications were both out of action. The ship lay utterly helpless, a floating hulk drifting down to leeward in the trough of the waves; from up on the bridge one could almost *feel* the blank inactivity below as all the familiar sounds – the pumps, the fans, the mess-deck radio – were succeeded by a deep uncanny silence.

The silence lasted a full two hours: two hours of prickling suspense, while over the length of the silent ship, powdered with a light mask of snow and rolling sloppily down wind, men sat and stared and cursed the slowness of the repairs. *Falconer*, who had received our news without comment, screened us all the time, circling quickly in a grim purposeful silence which probably masked a fuming impatience. We weren't much of a partner to string along with … Up on the bridge we watched her, and the snow-clad decks, and the guns'-crews standing ready; we drank tea, and talked (inevitably) of other breakdowns, and thought what a beautiful target we were making over this one. Down below they were doing their best, we knew; but if they didn't get the answer soon, we would have to be towed in – and the two of us, linked together and wallowing along at slow speed, would make a better target still.

But it didn't come to that. Chief and the Pilot (the electrical expert) did wonders with that switch-board, rigging up a Heath Robinson rewiring which somehow covered our essential requirements, though it was likely to collapse at the first harsh word. But it was grand to feel the ship warm up once more. The lights came on again, the compass started hunting, the fans worked up to a cheerful drumming which raised everyone's spirits. Even the morose Chief, coming up to the bridge to report, was now practically smiling.

"It's a shaky do, sir," he admitted. "But I think it'll hold."

"Any speed restrictions, Chief?"

He shook his head. "No, sir. It's 'Home James', as far as

I'm concerned."

That went for me, too … We passed the good news to *Falconer*, who broke off her screening manoeuvres and took up station again for the advance. As we gathered speed: "You did well," signalled *Falconer* austerely, "to effect repairs so quickly."

To which I replied: "Concur."[3]

By nightfall, after several hours of racing on together without result, our time was up, and we turned to rejoin the convoy – now three hundred and fifty miles to the south and west. They were already in trouble again, with a U-boat scare and more bad weather, and we were needed as soon as possible to complete the escort: this meant butting head-on into the wind and sea at a speed which I would never have dreamt of using otherwise. But *Falconer* (far better designed to endure this sort of battering) was the boss, and I had to conform to all that she chose to do. So we battled on, into the teeth of the gale, catching up slowly: even the few extra knots we could make against the tearing wind meant continuous pounding – a deliberate ill-treatment of the ship which I hated all the time. But with a flooded cabin, a broken rib, a piece of hot clinker which had burned the inside of one eyelid, and a series of electrical breakdowns involving in turn the lights, the gyro-compass, the asdic, and the echo-sounder (less important, at two thousand fathoms, than it might have been), I was getting past the subtler emotions.

Behind it all, of course, was the true debit – the failure of our excursion, with its ruined ship, its lost men, its hateful gain to the enemy. In that balance sheet, nothing else figured at all, or was worth a moment's regret.

---

[3] I met her Captain about a year later. He said: "I thought your reply so immodest that I had the whole thing framed and hung in my cabin. The alternative was a report to the Commander-in-Chief."

We had run for two days, and were within fifty miles of the convoy, when once more our plans were changed. The U-boat scare had proved abortive, and the convoy was nearing its destination: that meant we could be spared. Our new orders were to part company with *Falconer* and make for a Canadian port on our own. What was to happen to us there was not explained.

The first part was simple, though after five days of *Falconer's* robust companionship we were sorry to see her go; but our new destination set us a fuel problem which required a lot of working out. The port indicated was over a thousand miles away: our high-speed tour of the Atlantic, and especially the two chasing-up periods after the convoy was scattered, had used a great deal of oil: we now had to decide whether we could reach the new destination without running the risk of going dry. If there was a chance of that, our proper course was to make for the nearest harbour and refuel: if the chance was accepted, and we *did* run out in the process, the subsequent court of enquiry wouldn't take any excuses: ... I remember working out the sums with Chief and Pilot, over a table covered with charts, notebooks, and scribbled bits of paper, and weighing up, by calculation and guesswork, the various elements involved. There was the distance to go, the varying amounts of fuel used at different speeds, the chances of economising here and there: there was the possibility of getting held up by the weather, or becoming involved in some situation – a submarine attack, or a hunt for long-range aircraft survivors – which would call for high speed again. There was the question whether it was better to use more oil in a quick dash for land before the weather broke once more (it was still pretty rough anyway), or to go slowly and economically and leave something in hand to meet a possible gale later.

We made the various calculations, and set them side by

side: the decision I finally took – to make a fast passage, expensive in oil but giving less chance for the weather to deteriorate – was mid-way between the impulsive and well-considered. We would, at the speed I fixed on, use fifty per cent more oil than a slow crawl would take; but it *would* get the thing over quickly, and save a whole day at sea – a day in which anything might happen, from a gale to another electrical black-out. And if the worst came to the worst, and we were somehow delayed, we would just have to economize even further – becoming a sort of poor man's ship, shutting down one boiler, not using lights ("going to bed by candle-light," as Chief put it), cutting out the steam heating, not using the whistle … It could be done, though it would add to the normal hazards of sea-going something of the peacetime embarrassment of going broke on Thursday night.

Then, after twenty-four hours of head-winds strong enough to throw all our calculations out and ruin the whole scheme, everything relented at once. The wind dropped, the sea went down, the sun came out, warming the ship through and giving us a selection of cast-iron sights to fix our position by: even the ship seemed suddenly to be going faster than the revolutions warranted, and to be using less oil in the process … The last day of our passage, in particular – a run of 360 miles, in a sea as flat and blue as a willow-pattern plate – was the most delightful picnic imaginable, a holiday occasion which made up for all the doubts and difficulties of the past fortnight. All over the ship the hands were busy, working in the sunshine to restore the ship to normal – cleaning guns, touching up the paint-work, drying blankets and clothes along the guard-rail. It was one of those gentle, rewarding days at sea, which are so blessed a contrast to the general run in wartime; and to pass an afternoon up on the bridge, even surrounded by the thirty-five voice-pipes, the battery of telephones, the daunting array of gadgets, was to feel that there was something in sea-going after all, balancing the discomfort and the cruelty, restoring loveliness.

Next morning justified Pilot's admirable navigation; our course led us to the outer channel buoy, as straight as a die. We were met fifteen miles off-shore by a pilot-schooner – an old-time welcome which also blended pleasantly with the journey's end. Two hours later we were secured alongside, and the satisfaction of having brought H.M. Frigate *River* across the Atlantic was ours.

CHAPTER FOUR

"RECEIVED: ONE FRIGATE"

What we had brought her across the Atlantic for was not immediately made clear. I went ashore as soon as we were secured up, to make my number and find out what it was all about; but it was one of those occasions when the man you really want to see is out, the appropriate signal file has been borrowed by another department, the relevant papers have got stuck in an "in" tray somewhere, the Wren who knows all about the whole thing went on leave the previous day … I learnt nothing at all, except that they had been expecting us a week earlier; I imagined that they had mislaid a signal and couldn't remember whether we were to be refitted or attached to a Canadian escort group on this side for a spell. But it didn't matter much, for a day or so: I wanted a rest, I had never been in Canada before, and it looked (even in mid-winter) a good place to be in.

It was rough, of course: here was a harbour wrested (not so very long ago, as history runs) from an unfriendly countryside which seemed hardly to have become reconciled to humanity – a snow-bound rocky outcrop of a wild continent. But the waterfront presented a pretty and completely authentic air: tough-looking fishing schooners lined the quay, thick snow lay on the street and the hills rising behind them, people clumped around in a strange assortment of clothes, an endless variation on snow-boots, fur caps, leather jerkins, and multi-coloured lumberjack shirts. To me it was all new, except for what I remembered from Wild West and Gold Rush movies; I'd never before been so close to a place and people so obviously accustomed to living hard and keeping an alert eye on the weather and the change of seasons.

Newest of all was the sight of this lighted town at night – though it was odd to have to travel so far from "civilization" in order to find its most natural accompaniment. Not yet had our home black-out in Britain been modified; and the cheerful street lights, curtained windows, and shop signs were the first some of us had seen for many years.

They were an automatic lift to the spirit, as we have found at home by now: they give significance to community life at night, stringing a street or town together in place of the dividing anonymity of the black-out; and that first night, when the wardroom went ashore in a body, guided by the Gunnery Officer who was searching for the Anzac Club but finishing up in a murky dive which I hope had no dominion status of any sort – that first night was a cheerful tonic after the rough journey we had had on the way across.

We shifted berth next morning: a move made memorable by one of those remarks, overheard on the bridge, which chasten the spirit but which sweeten life at the same time. Misjudging the strength of the wind as we approached the quay, I put a sizeable dent in our bow plating. Said a brooding voice from the foc'sle below me: "I suppose if we were Japanese he'd have to commit bloody suicide now." … Then I went ashore, to be greeted by a real surprise.

"You're paying off," I was told. "Haven't you had the signals?"

I said that I knew nothing about it.

My informant waved his hand. "It was all fixed up long

ago. You're to hand over the ship to the Canadian Navy."

"What then?"

"You take your ship's company, go down to the States by special train, and pick up a new ship there. She's just finished building: you'll have to commission her."

"What sort of ship?"

"Another frigate, I think. Just as good as this one, anyway. Better, probably: she'll have a lot of new gadgets."

I said I was quite satisfied with things as they were.

He waved his hand again. (It was a good gesture: it covered everything – even a startling development like this.) "Well, there it is. How long do you want for the paying off process?"

I considered. Mustering stores. Adding things up. Getting everything signed for. Arguing about pattern numbers and oddments of equipment. "About a week, or ten days," I said.

Again that airy wave. "Can't be done, old boy. Five days at the outside. We've got some more ships coming in. Besides, the American ship is waiting for you, and you know the sort of split-second schedule they work to. Five days – let's say Thursday. Is that O.K.?"

I said that it was. I couldn't really compete with the wave any longer.

There ensued a glorious sort of picnic: but not the sort I had been expecting. Everything in a ship is listed, no matter what it is: when paying off, or on transfer of any kind, it is the usual practice to produce this list, and the articles in question, and tick them off as they are sighted. But the Canadians, God bless them, had a better idea than this – or perhaps they didn't trust our book-keeping; at any rate, their scheme was a brand new inventory, from one end of the ship to the other. Two supply ratings appeared and began to walk round the ship making a list of everything moveable they saw. They marched into my cabin, one with a notebook and pencil, the other with a sharp eye.

"One carpet, Joe," said the latter.

"One carpet," said Joe, and noted it down.

"One—two—three blankets."

"Three blankets." Scratch, scratch, scratch.

"Two pairs of curtains, worn."

And so on. I calculated that going round the ship piecemeal like this would take about three months. But it was certainly a nice homely way of paying off.

They must, however, have reverted to our quicker scheme, or got more people to work their own, because we finished the turn-over well within the time limit. The night before we were due to leave I had lower deck cleared and spoke to the ship's company about our future. I tried to make the morrow's journey sound something between a duty and a treat – which was what it turned out to be, with, perhaps, the emphasis on the latter. Certainly a long and comfortable journey by special train, with three fabulous American meals served to us *en route*, was not quite the duty we were used to. But I warned them also that once we reached the States we would *not* be holidaying: we would be there solely to commission the new ship and take her back to work as soon as we could.

Then I retired to my cabin, to seal the bargain with the cheerful Canadian lieutenant-commander who was taking the ship over. We got that bargain well sealed. Towards midnight he gave me a formal receipt for her. It read, simply: "Received: One frigate."

There didn't seem to be anything more to add.

CHAPTER FIVE

TRANSATLANTIC
LULLABY

To: James Kelley, City Room, *The Boston Herald-Traveler,*
Boston, Massachusetts.

My dear Jimmy,

Here's the letter I promised you, rather a long time ago
when we were saying goodbye over that last shot of Scotch
at Andy's. I'm sorry I haven't got around to it until now. But
we've been busy over here, as you know; and anyway, to tell
you what I really thought of America needs a lot more time
for reflection than you usually give your visitors. It was the
first question you asked me, before I'd been a couple of
days in Boston; it was also the last question you asked me,
just before I left. And now by heaven, I'll tell you!

But first, we'll talk about you. It was a lucky day for me
when I remembered the name of the man who'd reviewed
H.M. Corvette about two years previously, and rang you up
at the *Herald* office: lucky because you were such a grand
person to meet and go around with, and lucky also in the
America you showed me. I thought you'd be a lot too tough
for me! But that was only the first of a lot of mistakes I
made about your country, a lot of preconceived notions
which didn't last very long.

The immediate impression, of course, was of a standard of living – a standard of luxury, indeed – which we in England rarely reach and have now almost forgotten ever existed. Even in peacetime, your country would make this impression on a visitor; but compared with our drab wartime England, with its stringent rationing, its one egg a month, its synthetic this and bogus that, the things you were eating and wearing and using in America seemed to reflect a fabulous luxury. All the things we've missed so long – tomato juice, grape-fruit, meat and eggs and fruit and cigars – were there for the asking, and the shops with their unrationed clothes and really beautiful gadgets were a perpetual delight. (You ought to see some of our shops, Jimmy!)

Yours took some getting used, by the way; so did your restaurants. Figuring the dollars and cents was bad enough; but you'll appreciate the kind of problems we had to sort out when you consider that, with you, a biscuit is a cookie, and a scone is a biscuit, and another sort of scone is a muffin, and a muffin is an English muffin – and still nothing like it. Thank God, bread-and-jam was still recognizable.

And apart from this profusion in the shops and restaurants, all the homes I visited (yours included) gave this same picture of a standard of living and a degree of comfort which far outstrips ours; every family, except the very poorest, seemed to have a car or two, and a refrigerator, and a massive radiogram, and steam heating and conditioned air and a kitchen like the inside of a chromium-plated submarine ... Of course, man for man and class for class, you do earn far more money than we do (remember how crestfallen I was to discover that I, a lieutenant-commander with a wife and one child, got the same pay as one of your WAVE petty officers? That appeared to be carrying sex-equality, and a lot of other things, rather too far.) But there seemed, generally, far more to get for your money, as well as a terrific pressure on you, all the time, to earn more and more, buy more and more, enjoy more and more of these lavish riches. It was made easier for you to five this materially prosperous life; in fact in lots of ways, it was made darned hard for you *not* to.

But what places they were to visit, your American homes! Even though one was forewarned, that terrific hospitality of yours makes an overwhelming impression. Not only you, and the Captain's family, and my publishers in New York, but everyone I met, even by chance at parties – they all seemed to have this same generosity and open-heartedness, this determination to give me a good time and make me enjoy America. We all found it, whether officers or ship's company: a terrific amount of trouble was taken, not only to make us feel at home but to give us the time of our lives, on the house, for as long as we were around. It might have been embarrassing, because as you know we were all broke most of the time and couldn't return a fraction of the hospitality we received; but somehow it was done in such a natural way that this idea never made itself felt. Or if it did, it got brushed aside as irrelevant and swallowed up in some fresh demonstration of friendliness. It's something that none of us will ever forget.

That last phrase covers all sorts of other things, too: America was in many ways a land of continual discovery for us. Pretty girls, for instance. Your country must be a very nice place to fall in love (what did you say?) judging by the girls I saw in Boston and New York. It wasn't that they were all pretty, but they *were* all attractive; they'd obviously taken endless trouble over their appearance, playing up any good feature and being clever about the remainder, and it was really delightful to walk down a street past this moving frieze of faces and figures, each of which seemed to have its own cunning distinction. They were wearing flowers in their hair that summer – usually single gardenias – or little feather ornaments or velvet bows atop of one ear: the effect was enchanting, going straight to the vulnerable heart ... In England a girl is either pretty, or she is not: in America, she seems to have a third choice, difficult to label, but perpetually intriguing.

When I remarked on this, all you said was: "Don't you think the Great American Male deserves it?" I didn't answer that one.

I realized how lucky I was in meeting you in the first place, when I had a look at my American address list the other day. I got to know so many of them through you – you were generous with introductions, in the usual American way, as well as having an alarmingly wide range of acquaintances: and of course it led indirectly to many of the odd jobs I took on, to pass the time while I was waiting for the ship – the broadcasts and the book-reviewing, and that hair-raising speech to the six hundred women club-members which turned out such a lot of fun after all. (You work your writers pretty hard in America, between the radio and the interviews and the lecture-tours and the personal appearances: I sometimes wonder how they find time for anything as dull as writing.)

I found it pretty exhilarating, too, rushing round with you chasing stories. And what stories! The movies had prepared me for something of the sort; but that tough "police-court" atmosphere really is pretty hectic, you know. And I somehow got the impression that if the day's news didn't yield the right kind of headlines, then the drama had to be manufactured – I don't mean by inventing *stories*, but by painting every item of news much larger than life, and giving it an injection of colour and speed and excitement which it really never had in the first place. Reading the newspapers, it became apparent that there was noise and drive and crisis in almost everything that happened in America: all public figures were corrupt and flamboyant, all soldiers heroes, all brides strangled within three days ... Reading the newspapers, marriage in America hasn't just got its-ups and downs; it has tears, screams, sex-slaying, love-nest suicide, extremes of ecstasy and dejection, and smashing headlines all the time.

Remember how you played up that yarn I told you about our feelings after Dunkirk? Half in fun, I recalled that in my first ship we once had a rather morbid conversation about what we were going to do if Britain were defeated and we were left to our own resources; and the final plan was to take the ship to Canada or the United States, by a roundabout course, possibly sacking a few towns on the way and collecting food, oil, and bars of gold, so as not to arrive empty-handed. Once arrived on a friendly shore, we would, of course, become respectable again, and place the ship and our services at the disposal of the authorities ... But the written "story" you produced about it nearly gave me heart-failure. The headlines were quite enough for me: "BRITISH NAVY PLANNED PIRACY, LOOTING" ... Luckily, like all the best stories, it finished up on the spike. But that seemed to me to be a good example of a minor "good yarn" blown up to court-martial size, in full Technicolor. A lot of your life, and a lot of your news, and a lot of your human relationships, seem to have that same quality of hectic exaggeration.

And yet, and yet ... The real home life that you allowed me to share, and the time I spent with the Captain's family, were nothing like that: they were blessedly free of anything except the privilege of fitting into a quiet household and being accepted as a part of it. That was probably the best bit of America I ever saw,, down at your beach shack on the foreshore and staying with the Captain's family at their summer cottage; going out in the dory after lobsters (which *of course* are bigger in America than anywhere else in the world) or collecting and drying moss to make a few honest dollars. It was down at the beach, too, that I got my first introduction to the great American Sunday morning, with its sixty-page newspapers, its comic supplement, its late breakfast of orange juice, eggs, muffins, waffles, ice-cream, baked beans, coffee and doughnuts – most of it on one plate.

I think the time I spent down there, talking with you and the others, being educated about mint juleps and the correct temperature of drinks, and playing on the beach with those quick-witted and delightful children, made all the difference to my stay in America. I didn't just stay there. I was able to live there.

Of course, we got into arguments – plenty of them. I was homesick, and I was damnably disappointed about the delay over the ship. America was a grand place, but we weren't really entitled to our holiday there at all; and it was hell to hang on there month after month while other people were doing all the hard work, and especially hell to be loafing there on D-day, when, if things had gone according to schedule, we would have been in our assigned place at the landing. (You know, you don't know a damned thing about us, really – especially about our Navy and the part it's played in this war. I was in a taxi in New York on the morning of June 6th. Feeling pretty low, I remarked to the taxi-driver that I was feeling rather out of it that morning. He replied: "Never mind, bud—I dare say the British will have an invasion of their own, one of these days." ... I don't know the exact percentage of British ships taking part, Jimmy, but it *was* a British-planned operation under a British naval commander-in-chief, and we *were* there in large numbers.

(The taxi-driver got his ideas of an all-American show from the newspapers; and you can hardly blame him for that.)

New York, by the way, I thought was fabulous. Now

there *is* a town ... Your eye of course is used to these groups of huge towering buildings, rising storey upon storey with the traffic swirling round their base like the ebb and flow of a steel tide; but to see, for the first time, a place like Radio City – twentieth century achievement summed up in steel and concrete – made me personally feel I ought to be wearing a countryman's smock and carrying a straw in my mouth. I found myself gazing foolishly upwards, counting the floors and being nearly run over in the process ... There were other things to confuse and distract, too. New York seemed somehow to be the apotheosis of that side of American life I remarked on before: the dramatic, the hectic, the exaggerated. The buildings were insistent on their size, challenging all competitors, the coloured signs shrieked and blared and threatened, the passers-by were always in a hurry – clipping minutes off their journeys and movements in a perpetual rush to outstrip their fellow-men.

And yet there were quieter moments in this city which I can recall even more strongly. I remember looking from a hotel window across the unawakened city, at about five a.m., with the sun not yet showing but putting a lot of gold into that fabled silhouette. I remember the children playing round Central Park lake – a lake catching and reflecting all the polished scurry of Fifth Avenue within its circle. I remember concerts at Carnegie Hall, with supper afterwards at a restaurant – Reubens – which had such an exact nostalgic flavour of the Cafe Royal in London that I returned there again and again. I remember, above all, the Manhattan skyline seen for the first time from the Staten Island ferry, and a big convoy passing the Statue of Liberty, and the shattering coincidence of suddenly noticing my very first ship—the little corvette, *Flower*, manoeuvring like a self-reliant orphan against the unlikely background of Brooklyn Bridge ... No, New York was not all size and noise and rush. Your movies are bad advertisers there.

Once again, I was lucky in the people I met, starting with my charming publishers and spreading outwards in engulfing ripples of fun. That American hospitality, stepped up to New York standards, went into action as soon as I got off the train at Grand Central Station: everything was laid on – hotel room, lunch, the first six or seven dates, as well as a tough series of interviews and broadcasts which might well have got me snarled up without the expert guidance I was given. But by heavens, Jimmy, those New Yorkers have stamina! They seem to be ready for a party at a moment's notice, no matter how late it is – one gets the impression of people never relaxing at all, even in their own homes, but standing poised, in lovely clothes and exquisite hairstyles, waiting for the telephone bell or the ring at the door. And then off they go, to dig out more people, to collect poor old so-and-so who is actually sitting at home reading a book (a ridiculous thing to do – he must be ill!) and to start the party all over again. The amazing thing is that they look so well on it: you'll see them at work at nine o'clock next morning, as fresh as paint and already planning the next shambles. Whether they die young, I don't know. But they look, and sound, everlasting.

Of course, they're not America, are they? But what is America? Here's *another* bit of it I remember: another contrast, perhaps the most enjoyed of all. I was privileged to have lunch and spend the afternoon at Dr. Koussevitsky's house outside Boston, to sit in his studio (which has one complete glass wall looking out onto a forest) and listen to him talking, with exquisite understanding and wisdom, of the past and the future; to stay there until the evening, and then watch him conducting the Boston Symphony Orchestra with such profound artistry that one's only true reaction was humility ... Part of the greatness (and the oddness) of America is that Koussevitsky is not recognized simply as a musical genius: he is also recognized as a great man, and *everyone knows it*. When I gave his address to the Boston taxi-driver who drove me out there, the man said: "Say, that's Koussevitsky's house, isn't it? Are you meeting him? Gee, you're lucky!" "Are you fond of music?" I asked. "Hell, no! But he's a great guy." That's very American. I wish it were very English too, but it is not.

Well, Jimmy, how am I doing? I can hear you saying to yourself: "The boy's slipping: he hasn't started to pick on us yet." Don't fool yourself … Here it comes. I've kept it till the end, for no special reason: it will recall some of the things I said to you at various times, and particularly at the beginning, when I was fresh from the Atlantic and the concentrated war mood of England.

You know how America looked to me then. (I must emphasize that this was the spring of nineteen-forty-four, well before Normandy and the great Pacific advances.) You know also how (except in talking to you) I kept very quiet about this impression, for a lot of reasons: I was a guest, I was being royally entertained, and I had an idea that our wartime vision, in England, tends towards the exaggeration of anything which doesn't conform to our own stringent standards. But here, for what it's worth, is an honest verdict on America at that time, seen through a pair of British eyes neither more nor less discerning than the next man's.

I was there, as you know, a total of eight months; but after only a fortnight I had already noticed a sharp national division in your country, perhaps more apparent to an outsider than to some one nearer home. Already, in that short space, I had met two Americas: one of them was in the war, the other was not. Back in England, we used to have the same division; but it had by then almost disappeared, and the out-of-the-war minority was extremely unpopular – was, in fact, virtually outlawed. In America, I wasn't so sure: I had an idea that the ration-dodger and the gasoline-wangler were still looked on as rather smart fellows, guys who knew how to get along the right way.

That's why I've headed this letter "Transatlantic Lullaby"; it is meant to express the idea that some of your countrymen were not, at that time, in the war, and many more of them were still looking for easy ways of winning it.

You met that idea of an easy win a lot on your radio: the idea that victory could somehow be bought at the price of an extra war bond or two, and that you could salve your conscience that way. This seems to me about the most dangerous idea current to-day. We can win the war by working or by fighting, both to the limit of our strength: there is no other way, no short cut, no easier price-tag.

I heard a lot of funny things on your radio: I don't know what either you or your fighting men thought of them, but I know my own reaction, which was more physical than anything else. Some of your programmes, and the audience-reception of them, represented everything I am *not* fighting for. What did your men at the front think, when they picked them up on short-wave: what did they imagine was happening back home in America, apparently in the hands of youngsters whose every hysterical whim was catered for, and who were brought up on a diet of sex and the cheapest triviality? The fighting men were fighting: the people at home sounded as if they were having a rip-roaring time of it, as if even the Pearl Harbour headlines had not seeped through.

I went to a night club one night early on. One of the cabaret turns was a young man, dressed in the uniform of a private in the United States Army (the same uniform at that moment getting soaked in blood in Italy), who for a quarter of an hour gave possibly the most vulgar imitation of a drunken man getting thrown out of a bar that I have ever seen. In England, he would have been lynched by the servicemen in the audience. Here, they were eating it up – along with the butter and the meat which seemed to be available in unlimited quantities.

People who allow that sort of thing on the stage, people who find it funny, aren't in the war at all. They're in a private muckheap of their own making, directly opposed to the war effort, turning the whole thing into a sort of sniggering picnic.

I know there was the other side of it: I saw it, and I admired it tremendously. I saw your shipyards at work: I watched the work being done there on my own ship, and I recognized that it could not be surpassed anywhere in the world – that there, in America, there was a mass of people working intensively and courageously to win the **war.** But somewhere – at the top or the bottom or the middle layer – there was a kind of dead-weight of passengers, people who didn't know what it was all about, who didn't give a damn, who thought the war was a joke or a political swindle or a profitable holiday. I saw some odd headlines, too: "NOTED CLERIC QUESTIONS STALIN'S SINCERITY" – from the vantage point of the Copley Plaza Hotel in Boston. The war isn't just sitting back in an easy-chair and sniping at your allies. That is sabotage – rather respectable, Persian-rug sabotage – but sabotage none the less.

Understand this, though, Jimmy. Once again, I am one Englishman speaking, after a very short visit to your country; and I had my own bias while I was watching you. I remembered England in 1940, with the army straggling back from Dunkirk, with the bombs raining down, with defeat seeming quite close. I remembered our absolute unity then. I remembered the four years of convoy escort work I'd done, and being rather tired most of the time, and getting older with nothing much to show for it, and missing my wife and son. I remembered my friends dying in North Africa – and that without the benefit of Frank Sinatra. I remembered the two or three more years that the war *must* take, before it was over, and the fact that I should probably finish up in the Pacific, thousands of miles from home, with a valuable ship and a couple of hundred men and my own fatigue and nervous tension to cope with. Probably I even remembered, subconsciously, having "Limey bastard!" shouted at me on a street-car …

Yes, a certain bias might have crept in. But to an outside observer the fact did remain that, though a big effort was being made, it was not universal; it was being side-tracked all the time by foolish or trivial or catchpenny ideas and people: by people who thought it was funny to grab more than their share of what was going: by the man who was too smart to work one-hundred-percent, and the woman who was too idle or pin-headed to work at all.

A lot of you realized that, didn't you? One of the best evenings I had in America (or anywhere, for that matter), was that long session with you out at Watertown: when, reversing the usual roles, you told me what was wrong with America, and I told you what was right. It could hardly have been more refreshing – or more hopeful: there must be lots of people in your country who were like that, people who wanted to see that extra effort, that extra pinch of guts and awareness, injected into American life, THAT was what you owed to the fighting men: not an extra hundred-dollar war bond, not bogus morale-raising on the radio, not a promise that you could win the war outright if you'd only change your brand of soap flakes or smoke your path to victory the COSTLIER way.

There *were* a lot of people who saw the flaws and were out to cure them. There *was* a majority of men of goodwill—there must have been, for you to have made the tremendous national effort you have. And so, as it's all over now, I thought I'd mention it …

That really is all, Jimmy. I wish I could thank you

properly for the swell time you gave me. But come over here after the war, and I'll try to balance the account. (Scotch is a terrible price, though.) I've just bought a house of my own in London, and there's a room for you and Mary any time.

Goodbye now, and thank you for the use of the hall.

Nick

CHAPTER SIX

FRIGATE ALLEY

As a ship's company, we made our mark on America the moment we stepped off the train in Boston: I'll bet that's the first time that an American railway station has heard the sound of a bosun's pipe, followed by the stentorian order: "All hands muster by the bookstall!" ... It was six o'clock in the morning: returning revellers (as they saw in the newspapers) blinked their eyes ... Within about twenty minutes we were blinking our own, at the breakfast for 160 which the station hotel produced, without turning a hair, in one of its many banqueting rooms. It was the biggest acreage of grape-fruit and scrambled eggs I had seen for many a long year.

That agreeable introduction to America was only the first instance of a similar large-scale efficiency which, it seemed, reached every section of American life, from the supply of food to the building of ships. (In New York, breakfast arrived in a little cardboard box through a flap in the bedroom door: the box contained a thermos of coffee, two rolls, a pat of butter, an inch-high pot of marmalade, and a paper napkin. That hotel had 960 rooms: they each got one of these boxes, sharp at seven-thirty every morning.) The shipyard, where presently I journeyed with Number One, after seeing the ship's company settled in their barracks, had the same sort of all-pervading minutely planned efficiency. Whether you wanted a sixty-foot girder, a kedge anchor, or a paper cup to drink out of, they each had their assigned position, labelled in letters a yard high; all you had to do was look at the plan on the wall, and then pick them off the appropriate rack.

It was an enormous place, that shipyard: it had been a riverside swamp before the war, until Henry Kaiser came along and turned it into one of the biggest shipbuilding concerns on the East Coast. Certainly it was a monument to his fabled high-pressure drive. The acres of sheds, connected by wide roads and miniature railway lines, were in a spate of activity: the welding shops had enormous charts outside, recording the footage welded by each shift

We ran fourteen sea-trials.

in competition (I noticed that the midnight to 8 a.m. period was baldly labelled the "Graveyard Shift"): there were forests of cranes and derricks, there were whole chunks of ships waiting to be joined up, there was row upon row of assorted buildings – clothing stores, canteens, first-aid stations, paint-shops: there was an administration centre like a wooden cathedral … All these workers, women included, seemed to affect the same style of dress, a tough-looking blend of felt jackets, breeches, laced thigh-boots, and skiing caps: they looked vaguely romantic, in a workmanlike way, and a Clydeside dockyard matey would have seemed a very colourless creature beside them – until he got to work on the same job.

Number One and I were finger-printed, photographed, and issued with a formidable-looking pass and a lapel-button, all within ten minutes: we were then shown into a room full of depressed-looking British naval officers, all drinking milk through straws and making nursery bubbling noises in the process. The only cheerful person present was the officer-in-charge, an incurable optimist who to my certain knowledge wore the same gallant smile for eight consecutive months and always maintained, in the face of the most brutal evidence to the contrary, that it would all come right in the end.

When I introduced myself to him: "Your ship's waiting for you," he told me. "In fact, you're due to go out on your first trial to-morrow. Is the whole crew up in Boston?"

"Yes."

"You'll need the engine-room staff, and a few key ratings, down here by this afternoon. I'll fix that with the barracks: they'll be billeted here until you start living on board. Let's walk down to the jetty, and I'll show you over."

"What's the ship called?" I asked, as we set off.

"*Colony*" he answered. "Hi, Joe!" he called out to a villainous-looking fellow in a wild checked shirt, who

Frigate Alley.

answered "Hi, Commander!" and gave us what may or may not have been the victory sign. "There was one called *Montserrat*," the Commander went on, "which I thought you ought to have, but Their Lordships wouldn't play."

"Pity," I said. "But I suppose it's something to have a ship named after you, after only four years in the Navy."

He looked at me. "You can spread that yarn if you like," he said. "After all, there's one born every minute."

We strode past stacked rows of funnels, numbered and ticketed like top hats in a cloakroom.

"Who were all those depressed-looking customers in the office?" I asked presently.

"They are captains of frigates," he answered. His smile became more pronounced. "You may be a bit behind-hand with the story. I'll tell it you after we've looked round the ship."

Colony, when we picked her out of the mass of other frigates fining the fitting-out quay, looked very fine. She had the same overall measurements as *River* (they had used the British hull design), but the fact that she was welded throughout, instead of riveted, gave her lines a clean flowing look which I liked a lot. The absence of portholes (forbidden in American ships since Pearl Harbour), a lot of extra radio equipment, and some really beautiful A.A. guns, power-operated from individual directors, were the only external differences which caught the eye. But inside …

The refinements came thick and fast, as soon as we got below decks: a steam laundry, ice-water plants in each mess-deck, dishwashing machines, potato peelers, ice-cream makers, typewriters, two sets of cinema equipment – nothing seemed to have been left out. Meals were to be served on the cafeteria system, each man receiving an aluminium tray with two depressions stamped in it, one for meat and the other for pudding …

The internal communications were impressive: as well as loudspeakers in each compartment, connected to a broadcasting centre up on the bridge, there was a telephone system, with an "exchange" deep in the bowels of the ship, covering all the important positions. Nothing so old-fashioned as a voice-pipe disfigured the bridge: at action stations, I had a microphone with a wandering lead slung round my neck, connected to about thirty positions all round the ship, and the gunnery officer controlled his guns by the same system. But best of all were some of our "weapons"; the last word in scientific and inventive genius. "Looks pretty good," said Number One, eyeing the maze of knobs, dials, and coloured fights on the switchboard of a machine which told you everything about a submarine except its serial number, "though it'll never take the place of the old-fashioned night-shirt." But he sounded doubtful.

To deal with the extra guns and other equipment, our scheme of complement had to be amended fairly freely. When we finally sailed, it was with twelve officers and 160 men – generous for a ship of this size, but still only just enough to keep us rolling.

Of course, *Colony* was not luxurious, in the accepted sense of the word. The stringent anti-fire regulations which were the outcome of the Pearl Harbour disaster, as well as depriving us of our portholes, meant all-metal furniture, no rugs or lineoleum, and door curtains made of an unromantic glass fibre which melted to nothing when heat was applied to it. (My servant, not knowing this, tried to iron one of these curtains after washing it. He was left with a completely bare ironing-board and a scared expression.) But the labour-saving equipment, and the other refinements which went to keep us cool in summer and warm in winter, made up for a lot of this; and she was, anyway, a brand-new and toughly-armed ship, as well equipped for her job of long-distance escort as brains and experience could make her.

"And now," said the Commander, when we had completed our survey and were on our way back, "now, I'll tell you the snags."

I won't record his full story, interesting and colourful though it was, but only as much as had already appeared in the local press, where anything concerning this shipyard was reported with great freedom, including the names of all the ships, their dates of commissioning, and the difficulties which from time to time held them up.

Briefly, this whole class of frigates, except for one or two of the early ones, was hanging fire owing to an engine defect, common to all of them, which nothing seemed able to cure. No matter what was tried, it was the same story, with every one in the class: the ship went out on her trial,

We practised action stations.

the engine failed, she limped home and stayed in harbour until the affected part was replaced. Some of the men I saw in that room had been hanging about for six months already, with little or no prospect of getting away: as it turned out, we ourselves were held up for eight months altogether – eight months covering an exceptionally interesting period in the Atlantic, as well as D-day landings in Normandy which most of us had been looking forward to for upwards of five years.

There is little point in going into full details of our progress, either in the shipyard or later in the naval dock at Boston: but it was a sufficiently trying time for everyone. We ran fourteen sea-trials altogether, before those engines came right: fourteen separate repetitions of the same

In odd uniforms.

disheartening and largely futile process – out to sea, breakdown, creep home, fortnight in dock, and out to sea again. The earlier part of it was characterized by a jovial attempt, on the part of the shipyard, to maintain that the ship was really all right after all, that the figures must be wrong, that the strange noises emanating from the engine room was really seaweed lapping against the hull … It might have been amusing, a marine poker-game on a heroic international scale; but the ultimate stake was a lot of men's lives, and humour evaporated in a fixed determination that this ship would not be accepted until she was cured of a vice which was, at the moment, a positive guarantee of a breakdown in mid-Atlantic.

It meant a watchful eye, a measure of toughness, and a

certain amount of derision – most of the frigate captains found themselves being treated like mulish or ignorant children, at one time or another; but there was really no choice – not for honest men, and certainly not for sailors.

She did come right in the end, and I signed for her and brought her home. (I signed, by the way, "on behalf of His Majesty's Government" – an occasion not likely to be repeated unless there is some complex political change in the post-war world.) But in the meantime, here was an unspecified number of ships languishing in what came to be known inevitably as "Frigate Alley"; and here, on board mine, were 172 men with nothing much to do, hardly any money at all, months of frustration and disappointment to cope with, and ashore the tempting world of America, strung like a Christmas tree with attractions and luxuries they had never known.

I'm not saying that I had 172 problem children to cope with; for the most part they preserved an admirable discipline. In fact, what amazed me was the trouble they *didn't* get into. But certainly the situation raised problems which had to be dealt with, if the ship's company were to be kept together as a trained crew, and their sense of being a fighting unit preserved. Remember that they had hardly wiped the Atlantic spray off their faces, and had almost forgotten how to relax in any case. Since the beginning of the war they had gradually become tuned up to accept certain things which formed a cast-iron shell of discomfort around them: food shortages and difficulties, a total black-out whose effect, year in and year out, was immeasurably dismal, and a job – convoy escort – whose flat monotony was only broken either by action or by foul weather.

Now had come the release of tension, at one unexpected stroke: now they had crossed the Atlantic, and discovered America for the first time. They liked what they saw, but it *was* a trifle distracting. And there were other things besides the more obvious attractions, which tended to draw them away from the ship and the communal tie, and into a new world where they seemed to be privileged spectators.

To begin with, their uniforms, being foreign, attracted far more attention than they would normally do in England. People stopped and talked to them in the street: their opinion on all sorts of subjects were asked and listened to, from the election prospects to the chances of home rule in India at the end of the war. If they went into a bar they would almost certainly be stood a series of drinks – sometimes more than they were equipped to deal with. Back in England, they were simply sailors, and they merged into the general background of England at war; in America they were marked men, individuals who attracted attention and comment wherever they went. It was a nice tonic for the ego, being treated like visiting potentates; but 170-odd potentates aren't very good material for a warship's crew – things like cleaning out the bathrooms are apt to be overlooked.

That famous American hospitality was delightful – and difficult. In common with other British servicemen, my crew had, in America, a welcome of an outstanding quality; they were taken into their homes, they were shown exceptional generosity in countless ways, they were done proud. It was a superb tonic – but a tonic with a hangover; for it is not surprising that, after a night ashore when they have been given everything except the family jewels, they went about with a slightly dazed look for hours afterwards.

And that brings us, by easy stages, to women. They also were hospitable; sometimes in a limited sense, sometimes not. My job was not concerned with sex-ethics, and the moral issue didn't interest me, except from the so-called "Victory Girl" aspect – that is, I didn't want any of my men responsible for spoiling the lives of young girls, who would, in peacetime, probably be better supervised and more innocently employed. This was a problem in both countries, I know; we did not want to add to theirs. But it is probably worth remarking that, after some months in America, most of us were rather homesick; and the homesick man is a vulnerable man, for many obvious reasons.

The total effect of all these distractions was bound to loosen the bonds which fighting, and service side by side, had given us. Put down in a strange and, by contrast, luxurious country, treated with extreme kindness, entertained and welcomed on a plane which was entirely novel, we could not help but have our personal lives magnified, while the sense of professional and community effort was diminished. It was something which could be offset in various ways, of which hard work and counter-distractions within the ship were only two. But offset it had to be, if that feeling most valuable of all to a ship – the firm, solid, ship's company tie – was not to disappear.

Nothing of the foregoing should be construed as a complaint against America – that would be the depth of ingratitude. We had a grand time there; we will remember it always, and we went back considerably refreshed. But the drawbacks to that good time, in the middle of a war, had to be weighed against its tonic effect.

Of course, one or two of the crew did get into trouble – not that it's easier to mix with "bad company" in America, but the circumstances were so exceptional; and there was a good deal more leave-breaking than usual. We did our best, out of working hours, to substitute something for the lure of the bright lights – the film unit worked overtime, and we were able to send contingents out for harvesting on nearby farms – from which they returned far too exhausted to raise hell of any sort.

I myself had plenty of distractions: book-reviewing and broadcasting, running a committee to produce the perfect scheme of action stations for all frigates, and staying with that most civilizing unit – an American family – whenever I took some leave. Most of the others in the wardroom seemed to find an agreeable niche for themselves; and for the rest we wandered about in odd uniforms and tried to look as if we were just in from sea and off again in a matter of hours. After six months or so, the transparency of this became rather embarrassing: I felt that every bartender in town knew my face by heart, and every hostess at the Officers' Club was growing grey in our entertainment. Even the officials of the British War Relief Society – most generous of benefactors – must sometimes have felt that they were entertaining lodgers instead of casual callers.

There was, apart from all this, plenty of work in the ship, with her masses of new and intricate equipment; and we practised action stations and harbour drills till we were sick of the sound of the bosun's pipe.

Throughout this trying period, Number One and the Chief were towers of strength – of all of us, they seemed to be the most impervious to America in all its aspects; the Chief plugging away at his wretched engines, and Number One preserving an admirable, unruffled discipline, were like the solid enduring figures who walk on to the stage to conclude a dreamlike fantasy. Number One, indeed, was involved in a notable incident which showed this solid quality almost too abruptly. He chanced to come into the wardroom one day when we were still in dockyard hands, to find a welder carelessly showering sparks near a pile of shavings which might have set a lot of things on fire. He tapped the masked figure on the shoulder and told him to be a lot more careful, using a number of old-fashioned expressions which had not lost their cutting edge in crossing the Atlantic. The welder raised the heavy mask, and gave him a dazzling smile. It was a girl.

Just before we were due to leave, we had a fire in the engine room which had all the authentic trappings of disaster – red-hot plates, bubbling oil tanks, asphyxiating smoke – and reduced the weight of those of us who were closely involved by about six or seven pounds. But its rigours were nothing to those of attending the subsequent court of inquiry in the middle of a heat-wave, wearing whites which were traditionally spotless at nine o'clock and mere sacks at nine-thirty.

And then, suddenly, the engines came right at the fourteenth sea-trial, the fourteenth time of weaving up and down the narrow river and in and out of a dock which looked, even from a few yards off, about the size of a rat-hole. They had tried everything from bacon-fat to ice cream on those engines: one of the remedies, at long last, worked.

We found it as we had expected, a sad farewell, and we tried to temper it by giving a party to our many friends. It was, I think, a good party; but it produced a true story which I think illustrates all our American problems in one glorious example.

In charge of the cloakroom we had placed two men who were under punishment – that is, they were due for some hours of extra work each day, and this was one form which it took. As it involved hanging about for upwards of four hours, it was thought that it would be a sufficiently irksome fatigue.

Owing, however, to the generosity of our American guests, and their misunderstanding of the true position, the men under punishment made just over twenty-two dollars in tips.

As one of them remarked, not quite out of my hearing: "I can take punishment like that any time."

CHAPTER SEVEN
TRANS-OCEAN TWO

First stop, Bermuda.

It was fine to be at sea again, after so long a time out of our element; but finest of all to call in at this lovely island on our way home – a farewell blessing from this side of the world. Viewed from Boston, it was no more than a dot on the map nine hundred miles away, and it looked easy to miss; but as usual Pilot's pinpoint navigation put us exactly where we should be, at a very reasonable hour of the morning. Throughout the run Chief's engines purred innocently as if they'd never done anything else for months, and the trip was without incident except for a prolonged entanglement with some fishing dories off Cape Cod. At times we seemed to be rustling through them, like walking through a leaf-strewn forest, and some patches of fog were an additional complication. But eventually we drew clear, and settled down to our southward run.

We weren't hurrying over this trip, and we spent two and a half days on it, enjoying the long smooth swell and the weather gradually warming. Then on the third morning we came up – suddenly, it seemed – with this jewel of an island.

I remember that voyage round Bermuda as the loveliest run I have ever experienced. The hazy tropical heat gave the island a perfect setting, holding it magically between the burnished sky and the sea: the water itself was an astonishing emerald green, and the American destroyer which was a mile or so ahead of us had churned up a pathway of milky white coral sand. The sun caught this as we passed, and our own wake became a fluid luminous band circling the island: we might have been putting a spell round it. Not that it had need of spells: it seemed charmed already, with its brilliant green slopes and the white houses making a thin clean spine along the highest ridge. The pinkish coral reefs which fringed it, and through which we had to thread our way, were part of this traditional magic: even the tiny harbour where we finally berthed had the same sort of fairy-tale perfection.

The few days we spent there – the last of a long lotus-eating – were in some ways the loveliest of all. Especially, night manoeuvres in this setting, after a quick fiery sunset had presented the warm night for our enjoyment, shed all the ugliness and tension of war and became part of the same dreamlike beauty.

Then it was time to go to work again. We went far northward to join our convoy; as we went, winter came swiftly to meet us. In the space of one day we gave up our tropical kit, packed away the white suits and the khaki drill, and changed into the good old North Atlantic rig. Sea-boots that had been resting for nearly a year had their first airing – and wetting: all-weather suits and vast mufflers were dug from the bottom of kit-bags, disfiguring the elegance we had maintained for so long, making us feel like sailors once again. This was what we had all been missing, for a long time: the ship shouldering the water, the clump of sea-boots in the darkness, the cheerful clang of the bridge-ladder at the change of the watch, the smell of cocoa at two o'clock in the morning.

All through the ship you could feel this same spirit

stirring. The hands cleaning the guns and getting up ammunition whistled as they worked. The daily run-through of action stations and depth-charge drill was taken at a new pace which made even Number One look satisfied. Up on the bridge – intricately fitted, more like the control-room of a power-house than ever – the lookouts stamped their feet and muttered at the cold air: but they were really alert, for the first time for months, feeling that their job had some sense in it at last.

When we made our rendezvous, joined the escort group to which we were temporarily attached, and settled down in our position on the screen, we felt in full fighting trim; and the fact that we were the best-armed ship in the escort, with some weapons that these rustics had never heard of, completed this feeling of being right on top of our job once more.

We had, among other things, the very latest in Radar sets (built in America to the British design); and since the security ban on this subject has to some extent been lifted, it may be briefly referred to. Roughly speaking, this instrument presents, on a fluorescent screen rather like a small television scan, a complete picture of everything within several miles of the ship – the convoy shows as a compact blur of light, the outlying escorts are small blobs, the submarines (when they appear) are obvious intruders which soon catch the eye.

In anti-submarine work, it is probably fair to say that Radar turned the scale in the Atlantic: submarines were forced to keep submerged, after a painful period when their every move towards a convoy was detected almost before it had got going, and the sharp lesson which the U-boat packs received when they tried their normal tactics of surface approach.

Radar has, in addition, simplified station keeping to a ridiculous degree, since it gives you the range and bearing of every ship in the vicinity: it neutralizes fog, it pierces the darkest night or the murkiest rain-squall, it works as a supernatural eye, on guard all the time. Indeed, looking back on the old days in the Atlantic, when we had none of these pansy refinements and had to endure days of eyestrain and guesswork when clinging on to a convoy in foul weather, I sometimes wonder how we ever managed to arrive with any ships in company at all.

Colony was a grand sea-boat, though she still had that old wallowing roll we knew so well. But I think we would have been almost disappointed if she *hadn't* rolled her guts out at the first sign of a wave: it was so integral a part of escorting convoys, whether in corvettes, frigates, or destroyers, that a smooth passage hardly seemed to earn the money. To clutch the rail on the wing of the bridge, hung between heaven and hell, having the sun on your chin one minute and then, the next, looking straight down at the water a few feet below: to stay there for a long moment before lifting and lurching back again – this, at last, felt like the sea we knew.

The convoy was a big one; so was the escort group, which included aircraft carriers; and we had with us ocean-going tugs, a rescue ship, and a small convoy of landing craft which, tossing about like fleas on a griddle, looked as if they'd have given big money to be snugly beached at that moment ... I noticed, by the way, that we had a number of ships routed direct to Cherbourg – something new in our war, a prime development of all the struggles we had been missing.

The Battle of the Atlantic, that long and bitter struggle, was not yet over; but it was entering on its last phase, and this convoy, and the things that happened to it, were a close illustration of this. In the old days, given the same number of U-boats in our path, we would probably have had a running fight for a week or ten days on end, with losses of ships and men on every night we were attacked. This time we lost no ships – the air reconnaissance and the escort tactics were far too good for them. It wasn't that the U-boats didn't try; but they just didn't try hard enough – they failed to co-ordinate as a pack, they lost heart after one attempt had been frustrated, and they never came back for more. That was the Atlantic, 1944–45, in miniature; a winning battle, with the enemy aware of the fact all the time and putting up almost a token effort, as if simply to make things look all right in the deck-log.

I wish I could describe it in detail, because it was a pretty exercise in tactics on the part of the escort commander, including preventative sweeps by aircraft flown off the carriers; and the reconnaissance by shore-based aircraft was so frequent and so well laid-on that, in comparison with, say, 1941, when we might or might not have had the service of a stray Catalina or Steam-chicken[4] for a small part of the crossing, it made us feel like millionaires. Briefly, it had three phases, involving three groups of U-boats successively in contact with us; and because they never overlapped (another sign of half-heartedness) they were easy to sort out.

The first group was detected many miles off, by carrier plane, directly in the path of the convoy; but after one of them had been bombed and sunk the rest never even tried to get through to us, and we had nearly a week without another scare of any sort.

The second lot tried a bit harder, and for a time their efforts looked promising; they were able to reach the outer screen of escorts without attracting attention and they began to develop their attack about midnight. But a good guess – no, more than a guess, a skilful forecast – by the escort commander told him the side they *wouldn't* attack

---

[4] Sunderland flying-boat.

from (this was governed by the moon, the direction of the wind, and the last sighting-reports from aircraft): he then drew off some of his escorts from that side (ourselves among them), had the convoy alter its course away, and then put up such a tough demonstration of alertness and killing-power, including one attack later estimated as a "probable sunk", that the U-boats withdrew long before dawn and were never heard of again. None of them had got near enough even to chance a "browning" shot with a torpedo. With a convoy of this size, it could hardly have missed.

The third try was very much the same sort of thing, except that one U-boat, coming in submerged, did get within our range. But so surprised was he to find himself there that he lost his head and fired his torpedo in the wrong direction – not just a wide miss, but 180 degrees away from the convoy. For all I know he may be waiting still: the torpedo, when last seen, was heading sluggishly for the north coast of Spain.

There you have the Atlantic, towards the end of the long struggle, fought in waters where hundreds of our ships and thousands of our men now lie. Even to the practised and confident eye, it is still something of a miracle that a story which opened so murderously should have, after all, a happy ending.

We were given one more job before we were allowed to go home, and a superior job too: the escorting of a battleship up the Channel. This had a real touch of class about it, as well as taking us into waters which I for one had not seen since 1939: we were part of a destroyer screen performing prodigies of evolution, while the wagon ploughed a stately furrow down the middle. Our dignity however was somewhat marred by the following exchange of signals with the flagship:

She: "What are you?"

Us: "American-built frigate."

She: "Will you be our gum-chum?"

I could think of no answer suitable to a conversation between a lieutenant-commander and an admiral.

As we turned away, the job completed, and settled on our northerly course again, I had the "still" piped over the broadcasting system, and then gave the ship's company the shortest and best speech I had yet made. It was: "This is the Captain speaking. We will be home for Christmas."

But coming up river, and entering harbour, on that cold clear morning, meant only a breathing-spell for us: it was not the end of anything. We had been away nearly eleven months: it was the finest and most longed-for homecoming I could remember. But soon we would be off again, even farther afield. It would be the same sort of war: the water might be a bit warmer, and the prisoners dark and inscrutable instead of blond and unspeakable, but our slice of it would not be altered. Long-distance convoy escort was still the label.

There we were, anyway, passing the boom at practically the advertised time: H.M. Frigate *Colony* – American-built, British-manned – alert, seaworthy, and ready for the next round in the same full naval partnership.

Nicholas Monsarrat

The Pillow-fight

Passion, conflict and infidelity are vividly depicted in this gripping tale of two people and their marriage. Set against the glittering background of glamorous high life in South Africa, New York and Barbados, an idealistic young writer tastes the corrupting fruits of success, while his beautiful, ambitious wife begins to doubt her former values. A complete reversal of their opposing beliefs forms the bedrock of unremitting conflict. Can their passion survive the coming storm…?

'Immensely readable…an eminently satisfying book'
– *Irish Times*

'A professional who gives us our money's worth. The entertainment value is high' – *The Daily Telegraph*

Smith and Jones

Within the precarious conditions of the Cold War, diplomats Smith and Jones are not to be trusted. But although their files demonstrate evidence of numerous indiscretions and drunkenness, they have friends in high places who ensure that this doesn't count against them, and they are sent across the Iron Curtain.

However, when they defect, the threat of absolute treachery means that immediate and effective action has to be taken. At all costs and by whatever means, Smith and Jones must be silenced.

'An exciting and intriguing story' – *Daily Express*

'In this fast-moving Secret Service story Nicholas Monsarrat has brought off a neat tour de force with a moral'
– *Yorkshire Post*

Nicholas Monsarrat

This is the Schoolroom

The turbulent Thirties, and all across Europe cry the discordant voices of hunger and death, most notably in Spain, where a civil war threatens to destroy the country.

Aspiring writer, Marcus Hendrycks, has toyed with life for twenty-one years. His illusions, developed within a safe, cloistered existence in Cambridge, are shattered forever when he joins the fight against the fascists and is exposed to a harsh reality. As the war takes hold, he discovers that life itself is the real schoolroom.

'...the quintessential novel of its time and an indictment of an age, stands today as a modern classic'
– *Los Angeles Times*

The White Rajah

The breathtaking island of Makassang, in the Java Sea, is the setting for this tremendous historical novel. It is a place both splendid and savage, where piracy, plundering and barbarism are rife.

The ageing Rajah, threatened by native rebellion, enlists the help of Richard Marriott – baronet's son-turned-buccaneer – promising him a fortune to save his throne. But when Richard falls in love with the Rajah's beautiful daughter, the island, and its people, he find himself drawn into a personal quest to restore peace and prosperity.

'A fine swashbuckler by an accomplished storyteller'
– *New York Post*

NICHOLAS MONSARRAT

THE TRIBE THAT LOST ITS HEAD

Five hundred miles off the south-west coast of Africa lies the island of Pharamaul, a British Protectorate, governed from Whitehall through a handful of devoted British civilians. In the south of the island lies Port Victoria, dominated by the Governor's palatial mansion; in the north, a settlement of mud huts shelter a hundred thousand natives; and in dense jungle live the notorious Maula tribe, kept under surveillance by a solitary District Officer and his young wife. When Chief-designate, Dinamaula, returns from his studies in England with a spirited desire to speed the development of his people, political crisis erupts into a ferment of intrigue and violence.

'A splendidly exciting story' – *The Sunday Times*

RICHER THAN ALL HIS TRIBE

The sequel to *The Tribe That Lost Its Head* is a compelling story which charts the steady drift of a young African nation towards bankruptcy, chaos and barbarism.

On the island of Pharamaul, a former British Protectorate, newly installed Prime Minister, Chief Dinamaula, celebrates Independence Day with his people, full of high hopes for the future.

But the heady euphoria fades and Dinamaula's ambitions and ideals start to buckle as his new-found wealth corrupts him, leaving his nation to spiral towards hellish upheaval and tribal warfare.

'Not so much a novel, more a slab of dynamite'
– *Sunday Mirror*

Printed in Great Britain
by Amazon

58056087R00051